I Didn't Want A Divorce

Now What?

How to Deal with Your Ex and

Your Kids, Heal, and Get a Re-set

David E. Clarke, Ph.D.

With William G. Clarke, M.A.

To all those who have

suffered the agony of an unwanted divorce

ISBN 978-0-578-24566-9

Printed in the United States of America

INTRODUCTION

There's No Such Thing as an Amicable Divorce

"Our divorce was amicable." Don't you just love it when someone says that line to you? This person goes on to tell you that the divorce process was wonderful and hassle-free. Everything was divided up in a reasonable and adult fashion, the money situation worked out well, and the children are doing fine.

The clincher, delivered with a sweet smile, is the line: "my ex-spouse and I get along beautifully and we have an effective co-parenting relationship."

In response to this person's description of a pain-free divorce, you're supposed to say things like this:

"Oh, that's great."

"I'm so happy for you."

"That's the way everyone should handle divorce."

"It's best for the kids if you can divorce that way."

My Response to the Amicable Divorce

When a client gives me the "amicable divorce" speech in my therapy office, or over the phone in a phone advice session, I don't respond with the above expected platitudes.

I give two responses, neither of which are well received.

First, I say: "If your divorce was so easy and you get along so well with your ex-spouse, why did you get divorced?"

Second, I say: "I appreciate the effort but I'm not buying it. You are in denial. You don't want to face the terrible pain of your divorce. So, if it was amicable, you don't have to. I need to hear the real truth about your divorce so I can help you and your children heal and rebuild."

The Truth About Divorce Isn't Pretty

As a clinical psychologist who has worked with couples for over thirty years, I know better.

No one has ever had an amicable divorce. No one! Plenty of spouses say they have, but they are lying to themselves.

Divorce is the death of a marriage. It's the death of a family. It's the death of a dream. There is nothing good or nice or reasonable or amicable about it.

Divorce is a deeply traumatic, incredibly painful, heartbreaking, soul-wounding, life-changing experience for you and your children.

That's the truth.

It's the truth no matter why and how the marriage ended. But it is particularly the truth if you didn't want the divorce.

Now What?

You're reading this book because your divorce was the last thing you wanted. Your deepest desire was a happy, intimate marriage and an intact, healthy family.

The divorce has blown these dreams to smithereens. You're wounded. You're traumatized. You're shaken. You're depressed. You're fearful.

You don't know how to pick up the pieces of your shattered life, heal, and move on with confidence and purpose.

I know how.

My post-divorce plan of action will show you exactly how to bring order to chaos, deal successfully with your ex and your children, heal from the pain, and get a re-set in your life.

I'm going to help you build a new and better life. That's right, a new and better life. It's hard to see that from where you are now, but you can have it. God isn't a God of misery and hopelessness. He's a God of total restoration and a fresh start. He is a God of better.

The Authors

I have a Ph.D. in clinical psychology and a Master's degree in biblical studies. For three decades, I've been helping men and women recover from divorce.

My writing partner is my dad, William Clarke. He has a master's degree in marriage, family, and child therapy and was a practicing therapist for decades.

The Book's Target Audience

If you did not want a divorce, this book is for you. Whatever the circumstances of your divorce, you'll find help in my recovery process. But my focus is on these two scenarios:

Scenario #1: *Your spouse divorced you for nonbiblical reasons.*

You were dumped, rejected, cast aside by a selfish and sinful spouse.

Scenario #2: *You divorced your spouse for a Biblical reason.*

You didn't want a divorce, but you were released by God from the marriage because your spouse: committed adultery, was not a Christian and abandoned you, or engaged in chronic emotional and/or physical abuse of you.

You may still be single. You may be dating. You may be re-married. Your relationship status doesn't matter. You need to heal from the divorce or your unresolved pain will continue to damage your life and relationships.

Throughout the book, I write to the woman who is divorced. It may just as easily be the man who is divorced. Whether you are a man or a woman, my principles remain the same and my plan will be effective for you.

My Post-Divorce Plan of Recovery

My plan has four parts.

Part One: You Will Have a Better Life

I begin with a strong dose of Biblical truth and encouragement. You need to know you can have God with you in the recovery process and God is good with your divorce.

Part Two: From Chaos to Order

Your life needs organization, structure, and security. You'll build a support team, put new systems in place with your ex and your kids, and focus on self-care.

Part Three: Here's How Healing Works

It's time to clean out all the unresolved pain and trauma in your life. You'll take healing actions in these relationships: God, yourself, your ex, your children, others who hurt you in the divorce process, and those who hurt you in your life.

Part Four: Daring to Date Again

Once you are in solid recovery, you can consider dating. I show you who to avoid, how to find the right partner, and how to build a healthy relationship.

Let's Get Started

It's time to start our journey together to your new and better life. It will be three of us on this journey: you, me, and God.

Read this prayer of David:

> In the day of my trouble I
> will call to you, for you will
> answer me. (Psalm 86:7)

It is my prayer that my plan will be a big part of God's answer for you in the day of your trouble.

CHAPTER ONE

You Are Not Alone

Divorce has put you in a painful place. A dark valley. But you don't have to be alone. Two are a lot better than one, especially when God is the person with you.

Would you like to have God by your side as you go through my divorce recovery process? Stupid question. Of course you would. Well, you can.

Choose a Theme Verse

All the verses you're about to read tell you that you can have God with you in this time of trouble. And, you'll not only have God's presence. You'll have His power.

Lamentations 3:22-24 Because of the Lord's great love we are not consumed, for His compassions never fail. They are new every morning; great is your faithfulness. I say to myself, "The Lord is my portion; therefore I will wait for him."

Romans 8:37-39   No, in all these things we are more than conquerors through him who loved us. For I am convinced that neither death nor life, neither angels nor demons, neither the present nor the future, nor any powers, neither height nor depth, nor anything else in all creation, will be able to separate us from the love of God that is in Christ Jesus our Lord.

Psalm 23:4   Even though I walk through the valley of the shadow of death, I will fear no evil, for you are with me; your rod and your staff, they comfort me.

Ephesians 3:20   Now to him who is able to do immeasurably more than all we ask or imagine, according to his power that is at work within us...

Isaiah 35:3-4   Strengthen the feeble hands, steady the knees that give way; say to those with fearful hearts, "Be strong, do not fear; your God will come, he will come with vengeance; with divine retribution he will come to save you."

2 Timothy 1:7   For God did not give us a spirit of timidity, but a spirit of power, of love and of self-discipline.

Psalm 16:8   I have set the Lord always before me. Because he is at my right hand, I will not be shaken.

Philippians 4:13   I can do everything through him who gives me strength.

Read these passages again and choose one that resonates with you. Jot it down on a three by five card or put it in your device. Make it your theme verse. Read it at least once a day.

Choose a Theme Story

God wants you to know with absolute certainty that He will be with you in your recovery from divorce. So, He goes beyond the verses that teach His presence. He provides stories in the Bible that showcase His presence in times of trauma.

Naomi (in the book of Ruth) Naomi's husband and two sons died. She had no grandchildren and was too old to get re-married. Her life was over. But God, by bringing her daughter-in-law, Ruth, and Boaz together, gave Naomi a new home and a new family.

Peter (John 18:15-18, 25-27; John 21:15-19) Peter, one of the disciples, betrayed Jesus three times. Did Jesus reject him and not allow him to serve in a key capacity again? No. Jesus forgave Peter and reinstated him to a position of authority and respect.

Abigail (I Samuel 25) Abigail was a godly, intelligent woman married to the narcissistic and abusive Nabal. With her entire household under threat of death, Abigail took decisive action. With God's power she defied Nabal and the "wives have no rights" culture of her day. God saved her household, killed Nabal, and gave Abigail to David as his wife.

The Woman at the Well (John 4:1-42) Jesus should have had nothing to do with this woman. First, she was a Samaritan and Jews hated

Samaritans. Two, she was in deep sin (married five times and currently living with a man) and her life was a trainwreck. Jesus spoke to her, loved her, and offered her a new life through faith in Him.

The Chronically Ill Woman (Mark 5:25-34) This woman had been living with great pain for twelve years because of an incurable bleeding disorder. If that wasn't bad enough, her bleeding made her a pariah who couldn't have contact with others. She believed Jesus could heal her and He did. Jesus rewarded her faith by ending her suffering and giving her life a re-set.

The Starving Widow (I Kings 17:7-24) This widow and her small son were days away from starving to death. She had no support. No help. No hope. Because of her faith in God, God used his prophet, Elijah, to miraculously supply her with food and bring her son back from the dead.

All these persons were in deep pain. Deep misery. Deep trauma. In helpless situations with no way out. But God intervened. But God saved them. But God helped them to heal and recover. But God gave them a re-set in their lives.

God is ready and willing and certainly able to do the same for you.

Read these stories again and choose one that resonates with you. Jot it down on a three by five card or put it in your device. Make it your theme story. Read it at least once a day, along with your theme verse.

Here and Now Recovery Stories

I want you to know that God is still at work in the lives of those traumatized by divorce. I'm going to show you now how God intervened in the lives of two of my divorced clients.

CHAPTER TWO

God is Still in the Divorce Recovery Business

For over thirty years, I've been working with clients whose lives have been ripped apart by divorce. I could tell you hundreds of stories of ex-spouses who, with God's help and the right steps, recovered from the trauma of divorce.

I hate to repeat myself, but I'm going to tell you again: Every divorce is traumatic. There are no exceptions.

You also need to know that every divorced person can have God's presence and power in the recovery process.

To give you hope and encouragement and reinforce your confidence in God's role in your recovery, I present two stories of divorced clients.

As you will see, these stories are illustrations of the two scenarios I mentioned in the Introduction:

- Your spouse divorced you for nonbiblical reasons

- You divorced your spouse for Biblical reasons

He Divorced Me for Another Woman

My client sat on my blue couch and told me the sad story of her marriage and divorce. It was a good thing I had a full box of tissues because she cried her way through it.

After fifteen years of marriage, her husband dropped the bomb on her one night. She told me she knew their marriage wasn't great, but she was completely shocked by what came out of his mouth.

"I never loved you"

"We're just too different"

"I only stayed this long for the kids"

"I'm done and I want a divorce"

Of course, he failed to mention the zero quality, morally bankrupt woman he had been committing adultery with for the past five months. She found out about the adultery a few months after his I want a divorce speech.

She told me she was stunned. Shattered. Devastated. The feeling of complete rejection was intense. Her self-esteem was shredded. Her confidence gone. Her identity stolen away from her.

To make matters worse, she got lousy counsel from her pastor and a Christian counselor. They told her that his adultery was partly her fault. They urged her to chase her husband by losing weight, cooking better meals, and initiating sex.

This pathetic and unbiblical approach didn't work. It never works. It added to her humiliation and pain. And he still divorced her.

I got her in touch with her righteous anger. At her stupid, sinful ex. At her clueless pastor and counselor. At ignorant friends who blamed her and abandoned her.

She was also angry at God for allowing this nightmare to happen. I encouraged her to be honest with God, to vent her feelings fully and often with Him. She worked things out with God and built an even closer relationship with Him in the divorce recovery process.

She re-claimed her self-esteem, re-built her confidence, and created a new identity. She helped her children heal, got a job, and found a new church.

I Divorced My Abuser

My client had been divorced for a few months. She described for me -in detail, which is what I asked her to do- her twenty-year marriage to a narcissistic, emotionally abusive man.

He was incredibly selfish. Controlling. Critical. Zero empathy. Zero compassion. His needs were all that mattered. If something she did or said displeased him, he'd fly into a rage or ignore her for days.

Everything was her fault. She was never good enough. Her physical health and emotional health were steadily deteriorating. She saw her children losing respect for her and beginning to abuse her.

God guided her to my book, Enough is Enough: How to Leave an Abusive Relationship. She read it, followed my plan of escape, left her husband, and filed for divorce.

Her dirtball ex continued to abuse her. He wanted to make her suffer for divorcing him. He mounted a very effective character assassination campaign, built on lies.

He called her crazy....lie

He called her emotionally unstable...lie

He called her a narcissist...lie

He said she had abused him...lie

He said he had been a great husband...lie

His central attack was that she did not have a Biblical reason to file and divorce him. He got their pastor, their children, and some friends to agree with him.

My client was struggling with her decision to file. She had not wanted a divorce. She had tried everything over twenty years to change him and the marriage. She had a ton of guilt for the divorce.

Her guilt was weakening her relationship with God. She believed she had displeased him by filing. She believed God had moved away from her and was punishing her for the divorce.

She did the work of recovery and realized God was fine with her decision to divorce. She realized her guilt was false guilt. I explained the

Biblical support for divorcing a chronically abusive spouse (more on this in Chapter Six).

With God's help, she healed from the deep wounds her ex had caused her. She forgave him. She learned how to manage his narcissistic stupidity and stop him from making her miserable. She figured out why she had tolerated his abuse for so long. She did good work to repair her relationship with her children.

She built a new, happy life.

As I hope you can see, God plus the right action steps equals full recovery from divorce.

As you begin the hard work of recovery from your divorce, it is vital that you have God on your team. Not important. Vital.

Let me show you how to get God on your team.

CHAPTER THREE

Get God on Your Team

There's something you need to know at this early point in my recovery from divorce process. Here it is: *You will not fully heal and get a re-set without God on your support team.*

Without God you don't have the power to heal. You don't have the power to change. You don't have the power to build healthy relationships.

My recovery program is tough. Very tough. If you rely on your own wisdom and power, you won't be able to successfully complete it. You'll remain broken and unhappy and stuck in your pain.

With God, it's a different story with a different outcome. God will empower you to do the hard work, get healthy, and move forward with confidence into your new life.

To get God on your team, you have to do two things. One, you have to establish a personal relationship with Him. Two, you have to work to grow in your relationship with Him.

How to Begin Your Relationship with God

If you don't have a relationship with God, now would be a really good time to begin that relationship.

To know God, you must have a personal relationship with Him through His son, Jesus Christ. This is what makes you a Christian.

There is one God, and that is the God of the Bible. There is one way to establish a relationship with God, and that is through His Son, Jesus Christ.

Here is Jesus Christ, in His own words:

I am the way, the truth, and the life. No one comes to the Father except through me. (John 14:6)

A Christian is one who has recognized his need of a Savior and through trusting Christ has been forgiven. God sent Jesus to die for your sins – all the things you've done wrong – so that you can have a relationship with God.

This is what you must do to become a Christian:

For I delivered to you first of all that which I also received: how Christ died for our sins according to the Scriptures, was buried, rose again on the third day according to the Scriptures.

(I Corinthians 15:3-4)

When you believe these truths – Jesus died for your sins, He was buried, and He rose from the dead – you become a Christian. You have a personal relationship with God through His Son.

Become a Christian Right Now

If you are not a Christian yet, I urge you to become one. You can begin your relationship with God through Jesus right now by saying the words of this brief prayer:

Dear God,

I know I am a sinner. I've made many mistakes and sinned in my life. I realize my sin separates me from You, a holy God.

I believe that Your Son, Jesus Christ, died for my sins, was buried, and rose from the dead. I give my life to You now.

If you prayed this prayer – not just the words, but believed in your heart – you now know God as a Father, and He will be with you every step in your recovery from divorce.

If you're not ready to begin a relationship with God, that's okay. Keep reading. I hope that you decide to become a Christian along the path of divorce recovery.

How to Grow in Your Relationship with God

If you've just started a relationship with God, or have had a relationship with Him for some time, you need to do what you can to grow closer to Him.

I use the words "do what you can" because in your current circumstances, it will be hard to grow spiritually. The chaos, instability, and emotional pain you're in will make it a challenge to focus on God.

All I ask is that you do your best. Follow the spiritual action steps in this chapter and, baby step by baby step, you will grow closer to God.

You are Weak But He is Strong

You are weak now. Everyone has times in life when they are weak. I've had times of weakness. Many times of weakness. So, join the club.

Paul, one of the greatest and strongest Christians who ever lived, struggled with weakness. At one point, Paul cried out to Jesus and begged for relief from the awful pain that was tormenting him. Read the reply of Jesus:

> But he said to me, "My grace is sufficient for you, for my power is made perfect in weakness." (2 Corinthians 12:9)

Jesus told Paul He would give him the grace and the power to get through his agonizing ordeal. Jesus will do the same for you.

And, you will not simply survive this ordeal of divorce recovery. You will be a stronger and better person and closer to Jesus.

I want you to do six spiritual action steps as you work through my divorce recovery plan.

Step One: A Daily Quiet Time

This is you meeting with God once a day in a private, quiet place. There is no set time period. It could be five minutes, fifteen minutes, or thirty minutes. To grow and mature, every relationship requires regular time.

In each quiet time, I want you to do three things. These are my next three action steps.

Step Two: Read a Bible Passage

Begin your quiet time by reading a verse or two in the Bible. Use a version that clearly speaks to you.

I recommend you read a few verses every day from the book of Psalms. Particularly the Psalms of David, because you'll be able to relate to him. David went through many desperate, traumatic times. His Psalms are the honest, real, emotionally intense, and hopeful expressions of a man struggling to hang on to God in turbulent times.

Step Three: Praise God for the Victory

I was listening to Dr. Tony Evans (I love this man of God and his teaching!) on the radio yesterday and he urged his listeners to praise God for the victory before the victory has occurred.

Dr. Evans taught that praising God for victory on the front side is Biblical. Joshua praised God for the conquest of Jericho before the city's walls had collapsed (Joshua 6:16-21). Paul and Silas praised God before He miraculously released them from prison (Acts16:25-28). In many of his Psalms, David praised God for victory when his circumstances seemed hopeless.

Here's why I and Dr. Evans and God want you to praise Him every day for the victory He will give you in the recovery process:

- It is Biblical
- It will please God
- It will honor God
- It will glorify God
- It will be an expression of your faith in God
- It will draw you closer to God
- It will give you hope
- It will give you strength
- It will give you a sense of God's presence
- It will reinforce that God is in charge and He will determine the outcome

Step Four: Pray

In every quiet time, pray, which simply means talking to God. You can confess your sins, thank Him for all He's done for you and will do for you (this is the praise part), share victories and defeats, and cry out for His help.

Step Five: Attend Church

I want you to attend a local Bible teaching church every week. The Bible teaches that we are to be a part of a local church (Hebrews 10:25). You need to worship, hear a message based on the Bible, and build relationships with others.

Step Six: Join a Small Group

No one heals and recovers alone. No one. You need the support, encouragement, and practical help a small group can provide. It could be a weekly Bible Study, a Life Group, or a Celebrate Recovery group.

I strongly recommend DivorceCare. This church-based small group program has helped many of my divorced clients in their healing process.

Now that you have God on your team, the next step in your recovery is to understand and embrace this truth: God is good with your divorce.

CHAPTER FOUR

God is Good with Your Divorce, Part One

Recently, I talked to two divorced female clients in back to back sessions. The first lady told me that her husband had gotten tired of her and divorced her. He had a bunch of the usual bogus reasons for filing, but none were Biblical.

The second lady, after fifteen years of enduring an emotionally abusive husband, divorced him.

These ladies had two things in common. One, they did not want a divorce.
Two, they felt tremendous guilt for their divorces.

My job was to convince them that they were not at fault – not even a little bit – for their divorces. I'm going to tell you what I told them.

False Guilt for Divorce is Very Common

I have seen many clients – women and men – who suffered guilt and shame after a divorce that was not their fault.

They allowed their ex-spouses to blame them. They allowed their children to blame them.

They allowed pastors, Christian counselors, and others to blame them.

They blamed themselves. They believed God blamed them for their divorces. They continued to punish themselves for divorces that were not their fault.

Who's to Blame for Your Divorce?

Let me be crystal clear about who's to blame for your divorce. Read the next two paragraphs carefully. What I'm about to communicate to you is based on my thirty-five years of clinical practice, my graduate training at two seminaries (yes, I graduated from both), and – most importantly – the teaching of the Bible.

If your spouse divorced you for nonbiblical reasons, you are not at fault in any way for your divorce. Your spouse is one hundred percent at fault for your divorce.

If you divorced your spouse for a Biblical reason, you are not at fault in any way for your divorce. Your spouse is one hundred percent at fault for your divorce.

In this chapter and the next three chapters, I'm going to make the Biblical case for these statements of truth. These chapters contain the intellectual, rational part of my argument.

The intellectual level comes first and is important, but it's not enough. To erase all your false guilt, you need to heal on the emotional and spiritual levels. I'll deal with these levels in my *Here's How Healing Works* section.

In this chapter I will focus on those of you who were divorced by a spouse for no Biblical reason.

The Three Biblical Reasons for Divorce

There are only three Biblical reasons for divorce. Here they are:

Reason Number One: One spouse is involved in unrepentant ongoing adultery. In Matthew 19:7-9, Jesus states this reason. Jesus is talking about hard hearted spouses who were not sorry for their sexual sin and were not stopping it.

Reason Number Two: One spouse is abandoned by a nonChristian spouse. Paul, in I Corinthians 7:15, states this reason. If your unbelieving spouse leaves you, you are free to file divorce.

Reason Number Three: One spouse is being chronically abused – physically and/or emotionally

– by the other spouse. I will present the Biblical argument, from both the Old and New Testament, for this reason in Chapter Six.

If your spouse divorced you without one of these three Biblical reasons, then *he* is the one to blame – completely – for the divorce.

Of course, you made mistakes as a wife. No one's a perfect spouse. So, you are partly responsible for the marriage problems. But that is a completely different category from the sinful decision to file for divorce for nonbiblical reasons. That choice, that action, is on the one who filed for bogus reasons.

Here's the rest of my Biblical argument.

God in Malachi 2:13-16

God hates divorce for nonbiblical reasons and holds the spouse who commits this serious sin one hundred percent responsible.

Jesus Teaches that Marriage is to be Permanent

In Matthew 19:1-9 and Mark 10:1-9, Jesus teaches that marriage was designed by God to be a sacred, lifelong relationship. Any person who ends a marriage for nonBiblical reasons is a hard hearted sinner.

Jesus Condemns No Fault Divorce

In the Matthew 19 and Mark 10 passages, Jesus refutes the Jewish school of theology that taught a man could get a divorce for any reason at all.

Ending a marriage for selfish, nonbiblical reasons is a sin. Everywhere sin is mentioned in the Bible, it is completely the fault of the sinner. God does not allow the sinner to blame anyone else for his sin.

Stop Blaming Yourself and Start Speaking Up

It's time to begin shedding your false guilt over an unwanted divorce that wasn't your fault. One way to do this is to give assertive responses to those who blame you for the divorce.

Anyone who wants you to take even a fraction of blame for the divorce needs to be refuted. By you. Every time a blaming statement comes out of their ignorant mouths.

The one exception is your ex. Don't waste your time responding to his stupid, blaming statements. Ignore him and give no response.

But for everyone else, I want you to respond with confident, snappy comebacks. If you can't come up with a response quickly, it's fine to get back to the person with your rebuttal.

It's important for your healing and recovery to not take their inaccurate shots without responding. Here are the benefits of firing back at those who blame you:

- You don't weaken and hurt yourself
- You don't feed your false guilt
- You don't support a nasty lie
- You reinforce the truth that you are not at fault for the divorce
- You speak the truth, which is what the Bible commands you to do
- You are empowered
- You reduce or eliminate the blaming lies from those you refute

Dave Clarke's Classic Comebacks

Here are some edgy, honest retorts to those who attempt to blame you in any way for the divorce.

- I didn't want the divorce. He did.
- He had no Biblical reason, so God says it's his fault.

- Tell me what his Biblical reason was for divorcing me. Go ahead, I'll wait.
- Read Malachi 2:13-16, Matthew 19:1-9, and Mark 10:1-9 and then tell me who's at fault for the divorce.
- My mistakes as a spouse and his sinful decision to divorce me are two separate things. I own my mistakes, but I won't own his.
- Why is it so important for you to blame me? Think and pray about that and get back to me.
- Please show me in the Bible the verse that says a sinful choice is anyone's fault other than the sinner's.

Now, I'll address those of you who divorced your spouses for a Biblical reason. Get ready to start saying goodbye to your false guilt.

CHAPTER FIVE

God is Good with Your Divorce, Part Two

I never recommend divorce. I never have and I never will. That decision is between the person and God. I tell my clients who are considering divorce: "If you have a Biblical reason and God releases you from the marriage, then you can file."

I have had many clients decide to file for divorce for a Biblical reason. Not one has wanted the divorce. Typically, they endured their spouses' ongoing sin for years. They tried everything – talking to the pastor, Christian counseling, books, marriage seminars, lots and lots of prayer – and nothing worked.

Their sinning spouses were never going to file. These losers wanted my clients to file because then they could blame them for the divorce.

God Hates Divorce, Not You

God does hate divorce (Malachi 2:16), but He does not hate you for filing. God isn't angry with you at all. He is angry with your spouse for his sinful behavior (Malachi 2:13-16).

God knows the pain you suffered in your marriage. He knows you tried to save the marriage. He knows you did not want the divorce. He knows you had a Biblical reason to end the marriage. He knows it was your spouse who destroyed the marriage, not you.

If you filed for a Biblical reason, God is good with your divorce. God is good with you.

I know you still struggle with guilt for filing. I'm going to help you start the process to get rid of that false guilt.

"If You'd Been a Better Wife"

This is a lie that is alive and well in the Christian community. It has been used for decades to blame wives for their divorces, especially if they filed. Here's the twisted, anti-Biblical reasoning behind this lie:

> If you'd been a better wife, your
>
> husband would not have sinned in
>
> the sexual area or by leaving you.
>
> So, you are partly at fault for his

behavior. So, you had no right to divorce him. So, the divorce is your fault.

The truth is, your mistakes as a wife had *nothing* to do with his sinful, marriage-wrecking behavior. You were not responsible for his sin. He sinned because he wanted to sin. Even if you were the worst wife in the world (which you weren't), God didn't give him a pass for his sin.

"My Spouse was an Unrepentant Adulterer"

If your spouse refused to stop his adulterous behavior (which includes pornography, emotional and physical affairs, massage parlors, strip clubs, and prostitution), Jesus Himself stated that you had a Biblical reason to divorce him (Matthew 19:7-9).

Despite this clear teaching of Jesus, there will be some Christians who will still attempt to blame you for filing. Not just your ex, though he will certainly blame you. He has to justify his sexual sin. Don't bother saying anything to him about the divorce.

Here's how you can respond to the peanut gallery of haters and misguided nitwits who try to pin the blame for the divorce on you:

- Why are you focusing on my Biblical decision to file rather than his horrible sin that destroyed the marriage?
- How much sexual sin would be enough to justify filing? One affair? Two? Ten? How many times of him viewing pornography would be enough for filing? Give me a number.
- He's completely responsible for his sexual sins.
- Are you saying Jesus was wrong when He stated that adultery is a reason for divorce?
- Read Matthew 19:7-9

"My NonChristian Spouse Abandoned Me"

If your nonChristian spouse abandoned you by physically leaving you or asking for a divorce, Paul stated that you had a Biblical reason to divorce him (I Corinthians 7:15).

This is a black and white issue, but there will still be some Christians who will blame you for filing. These heartless, judgmental types will tell you that you should have tried harder, waited longer, and endured more rejection. They believe you never should have filed.

The trouble is, these accusers get into your head because you wonder the same things. Even though you had a Biblical reason, you struggle with the decision to get a divorce.

Here's how you can respond to those who blame you for divorcing a spouse who abandoned you (when you give these responses, you are talking to yourself, too):

- I didn't leave my husband; he left me.
- How long was I supposed to wait? Two years? Five years? Ten years? Twenty years? Give me a number.
- Why don't you care about the physical and emotional damage I suffered by being abandoned?
- Why would you blame me for his sinful choices?
- Read I Corinthians 7:15 and tell me what it teaches.

"My Spouse Wouldn't Stop Abusing Me"

The first two Biblical reasons for divorce (abandonment by a nonChristian spouse and unrepentant adultery) are almost universally accepted by the Christian community. Although you will still struggle with false guilt if you filed for one of these reasons, at least most Christians will agree that you had a Biblical reason to end the marriage.

Those of you who divorced a spouse for chronic abuse will not have the support of most of the Christian Community. The tide is beginning to turn, but those of us who believe chronic abuse is a Biblical reason are still a small group. Very small.

I want you – and I believe God wants you – to know that you did not sin in divorcing your abusive spouse. You had a Biblical right to divorce him. Therefore, you don't need to feel guilt for doing so!

Because this is a difficult, controversial issue, I will spend the next chapter presenting the Biblical case for divorcing an abusive spouse.

CHAPTER SIX

God is Good with Your Divorce, Part Three

I have a confession to make. Until recently, my position was that there are only two Biblical reasons for divorce: unrepentant adultery and abandonment by a nonChristian spouse.

I believed – and still do – that a wife has a Biblical right to physically separate from an abusive husband. I wrote a book (Enough is Enough: How to Leave an Abusive Relationship) with an escape plan for the abused spouse.

But I did not think that ongoing, unrepentant physical and/or emotional abuse was a Biblical reason to divorce.

Now, I believe that the Bible does teach that chronic abuse is a reason for divorce.

I did not come to this conclusion easily or quickly. It came after careful study of the Bible, consulting Biblical scholars who I trust, and a lot of prayer seeking God's guidance.

In this chapter, I present the Biblical case for chronic abuse as the third reason for divorce.

This is an outline, an abbreviated summary. To dive deeper, I recommend you read and study the pertinent Scriptural passages and consult these sources:

1. Divorce and Remarriage in the Church, David Instone-Brewer, InterVarsity Press.
2. Divorce and Remarriage in the Bible, David Instone-Brewer, Eerdmans Publishing Company.
3. Grounds for Divorce: Why I Now Believe There are More Than Two, An Argument for Including Abuse in the Phrase "In Such Cases" in I Corinthians 7:15, a presentation by Dr. Wayne Grudem on November 21, 2019 at the meeting of the Evangelical Theological Society. Available at waynegrudem.com
4. God's Protection of Women: When Abuse is Worse Than Divorce, Herb Vander Lugt, booklet published by RBC Ministries, www.rbc.org

Here's the progressive line of Biblical evidence for chronic abuse as a reason for divorce.

Abigail and Nabal in 1 Samuel 25

Abigail was married to a vicious, narcissistic abuser named Nabal. When Nabal's sinful behavior put Abigail and her household at risk, she took decisive action without consulting Nabal. As a wife at that time and in that culture, she put her own life at risk in following her secret plan.

God wanted Abigail out of this abusive marriage and He got her out. God killed Nabal to protect Abigail and end the marriage.

Though Abigail shattered the legal and cultural rules for a wife when she defied Nabal, God blessed her actions. God saved Abigail and her household and gave her to David as his wife.

Exodus 21:7-11

Moses stated three reasons for divorce in these verses. If a husband did not provide food, clothing, or physical intimacy to his wife, he was compelled to give her a certificate of divorce. This legal divorce protected her from an abusive husband. She was free of the marriage and could remarry.

Deuteronomy 21:10-14

If a husband became dissatisfied with his wife, he was not allowed to mistreat her. He had to give her a certificate of divorce. Again, this law protected a wife from a hard hearted, abusive husband.

Malachi 2:13-16

God was furious with selfish, immoral husbands who abused their wives by divorcing them because the husbands preferred foreign wives. God was so angry He refused to receive the offering of these sinful husbands. Clearly, God was on the side of the abused wives.

Matthew 19:1-9

In this passage Jesus mentioned only adultery as a reason for divorce. He was not teaching that this was the only reason for divorce. Jesus did not contradict the Old Testament reasons for divorce (denial of food, clothing, or physical intimacy) or Paul's teaching that abandonment is a reason for divorce.

I Corinthians 7:3-5 and 32-34

Paul implies that he agrees with the three reasons for divorce stated in Exodus 21. These

Old Testament reasons are, without question, abusive behaviors.

I Corinthians 7:15

This verse is the key New Testament passage that supports chronic abuse as a reason for divorce:

> But if the unbeliever leaves, let
>
> him do so. A believing man or
>
> woman is not bound in such
>
> circumstances; God has called
>
> us to live in peace.

The phrase "in such circumstances" refers to other painful relationship conditions, not just abandonment. One of these circumstances is abuse.

The phrase "is not bound" means you don't have to be tied to a spouse who has destroyed the marriage. An abusive spouse has destroyed the marriage every bit as much as a nonChristian spouse who has abandoned his partner.

Paul is saying that staying married to a nonChristian spouse who wants a divorce would condemn you to ongoing abusive treatment.

In the same way, staying married to an abuser would condemn you to never ending abuse.

God wants you to "live in peace." You certainly can't do that with an abuser.

So, Paul teaches that abandonment by a nonChristian spouse and other similarly destructive circumstances – such as abuse – are grounds for divorce.

God is good with you ending an abusive marriage because He wants you to stop suffering and "live in peace".

God Hates Divorce and Abuse

God hates that you had to get divorced. He knows you didn't want a divorce. He also hates abuse and the pain and suffering you experienced in your marriage. He loves you dearly and He did not want you to continue being abused.

The Bible, both the Old and New Testament, supports your decision to divorce your abusive spouse. You didn't have to wait for God to kill your Nabal. Just as Abigail acted decisively when she had had enough abuse, you acted to end your abuse.

God is fine with your action to divorce.

To reinforce the truth that you made the correct decision and to further erode your false guilt, I have more to say about your nightmare of a marriage and its aftermath.

CHAPTER SEVEN

Don't Feel Guilt for Divorcing Your Abusive Spouse

When I use the term chronic abuse, I want you to know exactly what I'm talking about. Here's my definition (taken from my book, Enough is Enough: How to Leave an Abusive Relationship):

A pattern of narcissistic, disrespectful,

and harmful behavior exhibited by

one person in an intimate relationship.

A Pattern

I'm not talking about one or two incidents of abusive behavior. I'm not talking about a decent, loving spouse who was guilty of the occasional insensitive action.

I'm not talking about a man who seriously sinned, but confessed, repented, was in recovery, and helped you heal from what he did to you.

I'm talking about a man who abused you on a regular basis. He started abusing you early in your relationship, and he never stopped.

Narcissistic

Almost all abusers are narcissists. Your ex was (and still is) a spectacularly selfish person. Everything he thought, felt, and did focused on one goal: to protect and please himself.

Your ex did not love you. He was only capable of loving himself. He did not meet your needs because he was never even aware of your needs.

Disrespectful

He mistreated you in a variety of ways, any of which qualifies as abuse. Verbal abuse. Constant criticism. Refusal to communicate. The silent treatment. Control. Anger outbursts. Substance abuse. Lying. The list could go on and on.

He may have been physically violent. But even if he never hit you, his emotional abuse was just as damaging and traumatic.

Your abuser had no conscience. He never felt guilt or shame when he hurt you. He had no empathy. No compassion. And, nothing was ever his fault. Everything was always your fault.

Harmful

He was breaking you down, day by day, month by month, year by year.

He was damaging you emotionally. He shredded your self-esteem. He took away your identity. You suffered depression, anxiety, and had no hope for the future.

He was damaging you physically. Fatigue, exhaustion, and a host of stress-induced physical issues were your constant companions.

He was damaging you spiritually. You didn't have the energy and focus to be close to God and serve Him.

"I Feel Guilt for Divorcing My Abusive Spouse"

Recently I did a phone advice session with a woman who had divorced her abuser. She told me: "I was married for over twenty years to an abusive man. He never hit me, but he emotionally abused me on a regular basis. I tried everything, but he wouldn't change. I finally had enough, filed divorce, and divorced him.

Now, he's blaming me for the divorce. He asks why would a Christian file for divorce when she had no Biblical reason? Others, including my children, are blaming me for the divorce. I feel so guilty. Did I sin by divorcing him?"

I talk to many spouses in the same situation. I'm going to summarize what I told this woman.

"Don't Feel Guilt!"

"Do not let this abusive, sinful man shame you. He is continuing to abuse you, even after the divorce. You had the nerve to divorce him and he wants to make you suffer forever for that decision.

You lived with the abuse long enough. In fact, too long. Your abuser was never going to change. He had years of opportunities and blew them all. Why should he change when he did nothing wrong and it was always your fault?"

The Guilters

It's very common, though sickening, to have many persons in your life blame you for the divorce. *Your ex* certainly blames you because he always blamed you for everything. He lies to everyone about you. He tells anyone who will listen that you were the abusive one, not him. He tells others, with a smirk on his narcissistic face, "well, she filed."

The fact that you filed fits his twisted, stupid, "it's her fault" narrative perfectly. He insists that you had no right to file.

Your children, especially your adult children, may blame you for the divorce. They're used to you taking the blame. Plus, your ex spent years poisoning them, feeding them lies about you.

Members of your family may blame you for the divorce. His family will blame you, but that's expected. Blood – especially sinful blood – sides with blood. It hurts deeply when some in your own family blame you. Your divorce is causing them to be uncomfortable and inconvenienced.

Some of your friends may blame you for the divorce. I should say ex-friends, because any "friend" who sides with your abuser should be dumped. Right now. These persons are calling you a liar and they don't care about you.

Your pastor may blame you for the divorce. He may say you had no Biblical reason to file. As we saw in the previous chapter, oh yes you did have a Biblical reason.

There's one more person who blames you. This is the toughest one to convince that the divorce wasn't your fault. This person is *you.* You are allowing your abusive ex and these other guilters to still be in your head.

You Broke the Rules for Good Christian Wives

These persons who blame you did not see and experience all the pain and carnage your abuser caused you. They all expected you to continue to be the good little Christian wife and stay married no matter what.

You broke the rules for good Christian wives by divorcing your abuser. Not the Biblical rules, but the old school Christian community rules. These unwritten rules state that you are supposed to stay married, tolerate abuse, and be quiet.

The sad reality is that, in many churches, even if your abusive ex had filed on you, the divorce would still be your fault. In these churches, marital problems are always the wife's fault.

Never discount the amazing ability of your ex to convince others the divorce is your fault. Most abusers are very persuasive. Brilliant, world-class liars. They come across as incredibly sincere because they believe their own lies.

Your Divorce is Legitimate in God's Eyes

You know what I say? Of course you filed for divorce! Of course you divorced your abuser! That was a healthy and, yes, a Biblical thing to do.

He was destroying you and destroying everything precious to you. And he was never going to stop the abuse.

Not that you require confirmation, but his continued efforts to blame you and make you suffer confirm that divorcing him was the right action.

Guess Who Destroyed the Marriage?

Your abuser destroyed the marriage, not you. Your abuser ended the marriage, not you. You simply formalized what he had already done.

Ongoing, never going to stop emotional and/or physical abuse is a Biblical reason for divorce. You don't have to divorce an abuser, but the Bible teaches that you certainly can do so.

God is fine with your decision to divorce your abuser. God knows that there are marriages that need to end in divorce. Yours was one of those.

God wants you to heal, recover, and build a great new life.

Stop the False Guilt

Stop beating yourself up for the divorce. Stop allowing your stupid, mean, lying, vicious, sinful, abusive ex to blame you for the divorce.

Stop allowing others to blame you for the divorce.

How to Respond to the Guilters

Here's what I want you to say to those dunderheads who have the nerve to blame you for divorcing your abuser.

Say nothing to your ex. That's "pearls before swine" (Matthew 7:6). He wants a reaction from you, so ignore him.

Give these responses below to all others who blame you. Give one of these responses *one time* to each person who tries to guilt you. If they try again, ignore them.

- So, you'd prefer me staying in the marriage and being destroyed?

- How many more years of destructive abuse do you think I should have endured? Give me a number.
- Chronic abuse is a Biblical reason for divorce. Do your research.
- Why is it so important for you to defend the abuser?
- My only fault was staying as long as I did. I gave him a million chances to change.
- He's a wonderful liar and he's fooled you. That's your problem, not mine.
- I've taken enough emotional abuse in my life. I'm not taking any more. Never blame me for the divorce again.

You don't give these assertive responses for these guilters – they're probably too stubborn or dumb to get the truth, although your snappy comebacks should shut them up.

You give these responses for yourself: to empower yourself, to speak the truth, and to not allow any more abuse.

Before we get to my *From Chaos to Order* section, you need to know some things that will make your recovery process more effective.

CHAPTER EIGHT

If You're Single, Stay Single for Now

If your spouse divorced you for a nonbiblical reason or you divorced your spouse for a Biblical reason, you are free to remarry. God's only condition is that you marry a Christian (I Corinthians 7:39).

Even though you are allowed Biblically to date and remarry, I don't want you to do either until you've completed my divorce recovery plan.

No Recovery Equals no Success in New Relationships

My client was married to an abusive wife. After years of tolerating her damaging behavior, he had enough and divorced her.

I helped him get strong enough to leave her. I helped him get through the nasty divorce process. As he and I began my divorce recovery plan, I urged him not to date.

He didn't listen to me. He met a divorced lady and fell in love very quickly. He told me she said she was a Christian. He stopped seeing me and dove headfirst into his new relationship. Six months after meeting her, he married her.

Six months after the wedding he was back in my office. Sobbing, he said he should have listened to me. He realized he had moved too quickly with this new woman. The new marriage was filled with pain, conflict, and misunderstandings.

Turned out, she was not a Christian. Turned out, she had an explosive temper. Turned out, she hated his kids.

I could have said "I told you so", but that wouldn't have done any good. I got him back into my divorce recovery plan and he did his work to heal and recover. Sadly, his new wife – who was also abusive – refused to work on her issues.

He separated from her and, after three months of waiting for her to repent and try to win him back, he divorced her. All the additional pain and another divorce were the last things he needed.

Reasons to Not Date Until You're Healthy

I don't want you to end up like my client. You've had enough pain. You don't need any more, especially when you can avoid it.

Here are my reasons to not date until you have finished this book and all of my steps of recovery.

My Plan Requires Your Total Focus

You have serious, hard work to do to heal, build a new identity, deal effectively with your ex and your children, and get your life on track.

You can't date and do all this work at the same time. You just can't. I've seen it done, but it's incredibly difficult.

My plan will take three to five months, maybe more, and none of it is easy. When you're done, then you'll be healthy and good to date.

You'll Choose the Wrong Person

Because you have not recovered from your divorce, you are highly likely to choose the wrong new person to date – and maybe marry. As my client did, you may select a new partner who is a lot like your ex.

You know what's far worse than being single and lonely? Marrying the wrong person.

Without recovery, you are wounded and vulnerable and needy. You're desperate for affection. For someone to find you attractive. For someone to care. For someone to make you happy.

For all these reasons, you are not able to think clearly. It's incredibly easy to choose the wrong new partner.

And even if you do somehow choose a terrific person who is good for you, your lack of recovery will cause you to gum up the new relationship.

A New Relationship is a Distraction

Falling in love – or into infatuation – is a powerful and intense experience. When you have been through an unwanted divorce, the power and intensity is tripled.

Because your marriage and divorce were so painful, you want this new relationship to be perfect and to help you forget your pain. So, you go all in and do all you can to make your new relationship great.

With all your time and energy poured into your new romance, your divorce recovery is put on the back burner. Actually, it's shoved off the stove.

All Your Unresolved Pain Transfers to Your New Partner

All of your unresolved pain connected to your ex – all of it – transfers to your new partner. You don't want it to transfer. You don't mean for it to transfer. But, it transfers all the same.

All your ex pain is now on your new partner. So, when he says or does something to hurt you, it's as if your ex said or did it. You experience the current hurt plus all the hurt connected to your ex.

This causes you to react very intensely to your new partner. It's an over-reaction driven by your unresolved pain. And until you clean out your unresolved pain, you will continue to over-react.

If You're Not Dating

If you are not dating anyone now, don't start until you're through my divorce recovery process. Wear a t-shirt with one of these slogans:

I Hate Men

I'm Not Available

Don't Even Think About Asking Me Out

My Boyfriend is a Hell's Angel

If You Are Dating Casually

If you are dating but there is no one special in your life, stop dating. Focus on my plan.

If You're Engaged

If you believe you've found the right person and you're engaged, I recommend you stay in the relationship, but get your work done. Go through my divorce recovery steps with your fiance's full involvement and support. He'll be a key member of your support team.

When you are done, ask your fiancé – if he's divorced – to go through my recovery plan. You will support him as he does the work.

If he refuses to do my program, break the engagement. He's not the right guy for you. If he says no, you don't mean that much to him. And, all of his unresolved pain will transfer to you.

If You've Re-Married

If you have re-married, follow the same procedure I recommended for the engaged person. You do the recovery work with your spouse's support, and then he does it – if he's divorced – with your support.

If your spouse refuses to do his recovery work, try the plan in my book, Married But Lonely. If that book's plan doesn't get his attention and lead to real change, get my book, My Spouse Wants Out, and follow those tough love steps.

At this point in the book, I've laid the foundation for your recovery. It's time now to start moving your life from chaos to order.

CHAPTER NINE

Create a Human Support Team

You must climb Mount Divorce Recovery. It's a tall, dangerous mountain with a treacherous ascent. You can't and you won't climb it alone.

You need a team of faithful, committed supporters who will help you get to the top.

A Human Team is Biblical

Christians in New Testament times faced many serious obstacles: rejection by their families, rejection by their communities, persecution by local Jewish leaders, harassment by Roman authorities, loss of their jobs, and physical violence.

Paul urged these new Christians to band together to strengthen their faith in God, to increase their love for each other, and to encourage one another. (Hebrews 10:23-25)

Choose Your Team Carefully

I want you to select team members who are one hundred percent loyal to you. One hundred percent committed to you and your well-being.

One hundred percent certain the divorce was not your fault. One hundred percent willing to provide you with whatever you need to build your new life.

There will be "friends" who say they can see both sides and who want to maintain a friendly relationship with your ex. Don't choose these types for your support team. In fact, drop them as friends.

Some support team members will drop out along the way. It will hurt, but you have to expect it. Replace them, and move forward.

You will need a human support team for a minimum of one year after your divorce is final. Two years is more likely the time frame. It will be longer if you have a nasty, abusive ex and children High School age or younger.

Lean Hard on Your Team

Don't be afraid of imposing too much on your support team members. Don't be afraid of burning them out. Lean on them hard. That's what they're for in this divorce recovery operation.

Tell each team member to be brutally honest with you regarding what they can do and can't do for you. A no is fine. A yes with conditions is fine.

What you don't want is for a team member to say yes to your requests and resent you for their choice to overcommit. Let your entire team know that you want to be told when they are unable to help you and when they need a break from their commitment to you.

What Your Support Team Will Do for You

There is a long and important list of actions your support team will provide for you:

- Prayer for you and with you.
- Encouragement when you are down and feeling hopeless.
- Money for bills, food, rent, mortgage, and other expenses. These need to be gifts, not loans.
- Help with your children in the areas of babysitting, homework, and mentoring.
- A go-between with your ex by giving him messages from you, dropping the kids off to him, picking up the kids from him, and working out conflicts between you and him.

- Fun, relaxing times spent with them and your children.

Here is Your Human Team

Family

Your parents, siblings, cousins, aunts and uncles, and grandparents should be on your side. If any are not, cut them off.

Close Friends

True friends are few and far between. These friends love you and believe in you and will do whatever it takes to help you.

Recovery Coach

One person, a close friend or mentor of the same sex, will be your main go-to person in the recovery process. Ask this coach to read this book and hold you accountable as you move through the process.

Pastor and Church

You need a pastor who does not blame you in any way for the divorce. And who is willing to come alongside you during your divorce recovery. A local church, as I mentioned in Chapter Three, is also a key part of your team.

Neighbors

Those who live near you can be a great help with your children, lawn maintenance, chores, and certain home repairs.

Christian Counselor

If you can afford one, a Christian counselor can guide you through my divorce recovery steps. Having an experienced and godly therapist will keep you on track in your recovery.

An Attorney

If your ex continues to break the divorce settlement by refusing to abide by the child sharing agreement, and by jerking you around financially, a good attorney will be required. If your attorney for the divorce was weak and ineffective, fire him and get a new, tough one.

Co-Workers at Your Job

Do your best to develop allies at your workplace. Your first year post-divorce will be full of challenges and life disruptions. Ask certain co-workers to cover for you when needed. You will do the same for them. Try to get your immediate supervisor to understand your situation and to work with you in your transition to a new life.

With your human support team being formed, it's time to get angry. Really angry. Let me explain.

CHAPTER TEN

Be Angry, Then Forgive

Here's a dialogue I've had with many recently divorced clients.

Client: It's been two months since the divorce was final. It was a nasty divorce. I'm fearful about the future. And, I'm very sad. But, I have forgiven my ex.

Dave Clarke: No, you haven't forgiven him.

Client: Yes, I have.

Dave Clarke: No, you haven't. You couldn't forgive him now if you wanted to. It's too soon. Forgiveness is a process that takes time and tremendous effort. It comes at the end of the recovery process, not the beginning.

Client: But my pastor and my Christian counselor both say I have to forgive him and to forgive him immediately.

Dave Clarke: They're correct about the first part, but incorrect about the second. You do need to forgive him, because God commands us to forgive (Matthew 18:21-35). But no one can immediately forgive someone who has inflicted serious wounds.

Client: Also, my pastor and counselor have asked me to write a letter to my ex in which I admit all my mistakes as a wife and ask for his forgiveness.

Dave Clarke: I knew this was coming. It's another classic Christian mistake in the area of forgiveness. Don't do that. This type of letter will weaken you when you need to be strong. You will own your mistakes and sins as a wife in the next phase of your recovery, Here's How Healing Works. In this current phase I want you to focus on his sins as a husband. To start getting your life back on track, you need to be a battering ram. Not a doormat.

Client: So, what is the process of forgiveness? What do I have to do in order to forgive?

Dave Clarke: The first step is to be righteously angry at your ex.

Client: I have to be angry? That doesn't sound too Christian.

Dave Clarke: Let me guess. Your pastor and counselor don't want you to be angry, do they?

Client: No, they don't. They are proud of me for not being angry.

Dave Clarke: They are well-meaning, but they are wrong. Unless you express your righteous anger at your ex, you can't forgive him. And, righteous anger is a Christian, Biblical emotion. The need to express righteous anger is both a Biblical and psychological truth.

I proceeded to explain to this client the critical role of righteous anger in her recovery process. The rest of this chapter is a summary of what I told her.

Definition of Righteous Anger

The Biblical, healthy emotional and spiritual response to sinful behavior that violates God's Word and does significant damage to persons.

God Gets Angry

God is angry in response to sinful behavior. I've already covered one example of God's anger: Malachi 2:13-16. God is furious at husbands who have betrayed their wives.

Your husband betrayed you. Get angry at him.

Jesus Gets Angry

Jesus is angry – really angry – at the Pharisees and he spends thirty-six verses expressing his anger at them for their sin and hypocrisy (Matthew 23:1-36).

Your husband is a sinner and a hypocrite. Get angry at him.

Jesus expresses extreme anger at the money changers because they are desecrating the Temple, a sacred place (Matthew 21:12-13).

Your husband desecrated your marriage, a sacred relationship in God's eyes. Get angry at him.

David Gets Angry

In Psalm after Psalm, David expresses honest, raw anger at his enemies. In Psalm 69:24-25, David asks God to pour out His anger at those who want to destroy him.

Your husband is your enemy. He has destroyed your life. Get angry at him.

Righteous Anger is Part of the Grief Process

When you follow the traditional Christian teaching and stuff your anger, you jam up your emotional system. You get stuck in the grief process and you stay stuck.

Your anger stays inside and keeps you in never ending grief. You'll remain depressed, fearful, anxious, and hopeless.

Every depressed client I've worked with has had to get righteously angry to get rid of their depression.

Once you clean out your righteous anger, you can move on to the other stages of grief.

Righteous Anger is Part of the Forgiveness Process

If you follow the traditional Christian teaching and try to forgive without expressing your righteous anger, you won't get anywhere near forgiveness. You will remain wounded and bitter at your ex and others who have harmed you.

I've worked with clients who refused to properly express their righteous anger. In addition to being stuck in depression and grief, they remained bitter at their ex-spouses for decades.

One "stuck" client actually went to her ex's funeral and told everyone there who would listen how awful he had been as a husband. This was a man she had divorced ten years earlier! Pathetic, but that's what unexpressed anger can do to you.

Righteous Anger is a Healthy Response to Trauma

The serious sin of your ex has traumatized you. Righteous anger is a God-designed response to that trauma. Your anger will give you the energy and motivation to do the hard work of recovery.

Warn your Support Team that you will be getting angry, righteously angry, as part of your healing journey. You will be edgy, irritable, and they'll witness you over-reacting to any perceived hurts.

If any members of your Support Team can't handle your anger and want you to stuff it, respectfully kick them off your team.

In this phase of recovery, From Chaos to Order, I want you to get righteously angry at your ex and others who gouged you in the divorce process.

You're thinking, "but how do I get righteously angry?" I'm glad you asked. If you haven't picked up on this yet, I'm a master at getting people angry.

Let's start getting you angry.

CHAPTER ELEVEN

How to Get Righteously Angry

Time alone doesn't heal you. In fact, your situation will get worse over time if you don't heal in a healthy way. Each step in my divorce recovery process has to be done in the right order and in the right way.

It doesn't matter if your divorce was weeks, months, or years ago. If you skipped the righteous anger step or didn't do it properly, you have to go back and do it right.

Three Things You Need to Know

First, when I use the word anger in this chapter, I mean righteous anger.

Second, you are not cleaning your anger out of your emotional system in this phase. You are connecting to your anger, holding onto it, and using it to get your life on track. (In the next section, Here's How Healing Works, I'll help you get rid of your anger and forgive.)

Just as David did in many of his Psalms, you are going to stay angry until you have accomplished what needs to be done.

Third, I want you to focus only on your ex-spouse in this anger phase. There are certainly others who wounded you during the marriage and divorce process, but we'll deal with these persons in the Healing Section.

The Top Three Insults

List the top three things your ex did to you that caused the most pain. Don't use general categories. I want specific events in time.

Here are the Top Three Insults of one of my divorced clients:

#1: The night you told me you wanted a divorce.

#2: The morning I discovered your adultery.

#3: Our last couple counseling session.

Re-Live Each Insult

Talk through each Insult, using as much detail as possible, with two Support Team Members: God and Your Recovery Coach. If you are seeing a Christian counselor, talk about each Insult with this professional also.

Pray before each of these angry rants – and they are rants – that God will get you in touch with your anger and help you fully express it. He'll answer these prayers.

The verbal expression of painful events with a supportive listener will get you in touch with your anger.

Go Full Throttle with Your Anger

Don't hold back. Give full, spontaneous, unrestrained expression of your anger. Go over every detail of the Three Insults because your anger is attached to the details.

Don't be afraid you will get too angry and lose control. You can't be too angry. And you won't lose control. Persons who stuff their anger are the ones that lose control.

Follow David's example in his Psalms and vent your heart out with no restrictions. Pump out your raw, visceral rage at your ex. Show no mercy. No compassion. No understanding or excusing his sinful behavior. No forgiveness offered – not even a little bit. Not now.

You are ranting because you need to rant. Some things are worth ranting about. Being rejected, emotionally abused, and forced into a divorce you didn't want are worth ranting about.

One Partial Rant

Here's part of an Insult Rant one of my divorced clients delivered in my therapy office:

> I will never forget the night he told
>
> me he wanted to divorce me. I had
>
> no idea the bomb was coming. He
>
> never talked much in our marriage
>
> and hardly ever shared anything
>
> personal. He chose that night,
>
> September 22, at 9:30PM, to finally
>
> open up. Too bad it was to inform
>
> me that he was going to divorce me.
>
> He gave me incredibly lame, stupid
>
> excuses to end our marriage and
>
> break my heart and the hearts of our
>
> children. That's because he's stupid,

probably the stupidest man on earth.

"I don't love you anymore", he said.

"It's better for the children", he said.

"I want to be happy", he said. Really? That's the best he could do? What an idiot!

I was shocked back then. I'm angry now, angrier than I have ever been in my life. He is a sinful, selfish, evil man! I hate his guts.

She ranted for about twenty minutes, but this brief part of her monologue gives you a flavor for what I want you to do.

More and More Anger

Each time you verbalize your anger to God and your Recovery Coach, more details about the event will emerge. And, more and more of your anger will bubble up. You'll be surprised at what will come out of your mouth.

By the time you've ranted about your Top Three Insults to God and your Recovery Coach, your healthy, justified, righteous anger will be at full throttle.

Vent to the Empty Chair

Once you have vented to your two Support Team members, I want you to vent your anger about your Three Insults directly to your ex.

Not in person, by email, by phone, or by text. In fact, I don't want you to ever communicate your anger (or any of your wounded feelings) to your ex. This would simply cause you more pain, and you've had enough pain from him.

If you shared your anger with your ex, he'd hurt you again by: laughing at you, blaming you, contradicting you, or ignoring you.

What I want you to do is find a private, quiet room with two chairs in it. You sit in one chair and you put your ex in the empty chair. Then, you blast him with your anger for the Three Insults he inflicted upon you.

Psychologically, after about two minutes, it's just as if your ex is actually in the chair. God will make the scene real.

You can do the empty chair rant alone or in front of your Recovery Coach or Christian Therapist.

Tell him, mano a mano, what you think of him and his hateful, marriage destroying behavior. Turn the firehose of your righteous rage on him and pin his wretched carcass of a body to the back of his chair.

One Partial Empty Chair Rant

Here's a brief part of one divorced client's empty chair rant of rage in my office:

That morning, last June, all I was

going to do was check your phone

for a receipt. Suddenly, and I know it

was God, I saw your texts to your

skank of a co-worker.

I read the flirty, loving, sweet things

you texted to her. Things I longed to

hear from you but rarely did. And

her nauseating texts to you.

I felt shocked, humiliated, and

rejected. Ugly. Worthless. I'm over

those feelings now, you pathetic

adulterer. You cheated, lied, and

you ruined our family.

I hate you and am not sorry for

hating you. You deserve to be hated.

I'd call you scum of the earth but

that wouldn't be fair to scum

everywhere.

You can cover all Three Insults in one sitting, or at separate sittings. If you are blocking on getting fully in touch with your anger, do all three in one sitting. An extended rant on all Three to your ex in the chair can breakthrough to your anger.

Record Your Three Insults

To stay connected to your righteous anger, record your Insults in your phone or other electronic device. Or, jot them down on a 3X5 card. When you sense your anger weakening, read over the list.

With your righteous anger energized, you can take effective action to reclaim stability in your life.

CHAPTER TWELVE

It's a Whole New World

You've had enough chaos and uncertainty. It's time for order and security. You need to get your life back into some kind of coherent shape.

You must build a new identity. A new life. A new you.

Let's get started on your new normal.

Your Home

It's best to get out of the home you shared with your ex. Too many memories. Thanks to him, you're starting over. So, a fresh start in a new place makes sense.

If you can't leave your old home yet, change it up inside and out. This is Spring Cleaning on steroids. Move the furniture around. Paint. Put up new pictures. Put down new throw rugs. Get new towels. Move into a different bedroom, or move the bed to a new spot in your bedroom.

Change the locks. If you have an automatic garage door, put in a new code. Your house is your place of safety and sanctuary. Don't let your ex come one foot inside it.

Your Church

After the divorce, you may be able to stay at your church. If your pastor was very supportive, if the majority of your church friends are on your side, and if your ex goes to another church, staying makes sense.

But if any of the above conditions isn't true, you're better off finding a new church. If your ex was popular at your church, chances are good that he'll win in the public relations arena. You don't have the time or the energy to correct all the lies he's told to the leaders and members of your church.

Keep in mind that, regardless of how the marriage ended, many of the Christians who knew you and your ex will blame you for the divorce.

Just as your old home does, your church has many memories. These memories, good and bad, can make it difficult to worship there.

Pray about leaving your church. If your pastor is supportive, talk to him about it. It may be best to find a new church where no one knows you and your ex.

Your Finances

Money is going to be tight. Probably very tight. Divorce does great damage to every area of your life, including finances.

Sit down with a financial advisor and take a hard, realistic look at your money situation. Ask your Support Team and your pastor for the name of an advisor who will help you for free or at a reduced rate.

With the advisor's guidance, develop a budget. Create a savings plan, even if you can contribute only a small amount each month. Carry the right type and amount of insurance. Figure out how to deal with your debt.

You may have to make serious cuts in a number of areas: cable television, eating out, vacations, coffee, buying clothes. You may have to trade in your car for a less expensive vehicle.

Contact the Dave Ramsey organization and ask them for guidance. He is the number one Christian financial advisor in the world and has many resources.

Your Career

You may need to get a job. You may need to get a new job which pays more and has a more flexible schedule. You may need more education or training to get the job you want.

Lean on your Support Team for guidance and job information. Work every contact, every person you know, for help in the career area.

Your Friends

Expect to lose most, if not all, of your couple friends. They did things with you and your ex. So, now that it's just you, it will be super awkward and the relationship dynamics don't work.

In a few cases, one or two, you may be able to maintain a close relationship with the wife of a couple. If she is on your side, loves you, and is good with spending one on one time with you, the relationship will work.

As I mentioned before, dump any "friend" who blames you in any way for the divorce. And, dump any "friend" who maintains a relationship with your ex.

Part of the new you will be making new friends.

Your Self-Care

You have to learn how to take care of yourself. Believe me, no one else will. Your Support Team will help you, but there are limits to what they can do for you.

You spent years thinking of your ex, meeting his needs. Serving him. Supporting him. Trying to please him. If you have children, you certainly expended a lot of energy and time meeting their needs.

While you will still take care of the children, it's time now to think of yourself. To meet your own needs. This will feel selfish. It's not. It's healthy.

Self-care, which is a form of self-love, is Biblical:

> Jesus replied: 'Love the Lord your God
>
> with all your heart and with all your
>
> soul and with all your mind. This is the
>
> first and greatest commandment. And
>
> the second is like it: Love your

neighbor as yourself.'

(Matthew 22:37-39)

Though most Bible commentators ignore the "as yourself" phrase, it is clear that Jesus is commanding us to love ourselves.

The truth is, if you don't love yourself in a healthy way, you will be unable to love anyone else in a healthy way.

Diet and Exercise

You know what I'm going to tell you to do. Everyone on planet earth knows it. You just have to do it.

Eat healthy food. Plenty of vegetables. Less sugary snacks. If you need to lose weight, now is the time to do it. You certainly don't do it for your ex. You do it for yourself.

Develop a regular exercise program and stick to it. Don't overdo it. You are not training for the Olympics. Walk. Swim. Do the exercise bike. Sit ups. Push ups. Go to a gym if that's your thing.

You desperately need the strength, confidence, endurance, energy, and discipline that comes from a healthy diet and regular exercise.

Say No

Most of my divorced clients have hardly ever said the word "no". They are used to saying "yes" to just about everyone in their lives. That has to change after divorce. Post-divorce is survival time and "no" needs to come out of your previously sweet mouth a lot more.

Say no to your kid's teachers. Say no to serving in the church. Say no to any family or social events that will drain your energy. Say no to extra tasks at work that no one is paying you to do.

Say no to your kids if what they're asking costs too much or will push you over the edge emotionally or physically. Say no to your own family if needed. Say no to your in-laws when they ask to see your kids, unless it is a genuine help to you.

If your in-laws wounded you in the divorce process, don't let them see your kids when it's your time with them. They can see the kids on your ex's time.

Have Fun

In the midst of the post-divorce nightmare, you need to hang on to activities and hobbies that you enjoy. You will have less time to engage in these activities, but even a few minutes of fun is stress-reducing and life-giving.

Your children are precious to you. A key element in bringing order to your new life is handling your children in an effective, healthy way.

CHAPTER THIRTEEN

You and Your Younger Children

I just finished a phone advice session with a recently divorced woman. I told her she was making a critical mistake in her post-divorce parenting. It was a common and understandable mistake, but a mistake nonetheless.

She wanted vindication in the eyes of her children.

- She wanted her children to understand the terrible pain their father had caused her during the marriage and the divorce.
- She wanted her children to be angry, as angry as she was, at their father.
- She wanted her children to be on her side.
- She wanted her children to be closer to her than to their father.

To achieve these goals, she was telling the children the details of their father's hurtful actions during the marriage and divorce. She was expressing her anger and deep hurt to the children and leaning on them for emotional support.

She was limiting her ex's ability to communicate with the children. She was asking them to not spend time with their father. She was pressing the children to cut off their father and only have a relationship with her.

I told her to stop this approach. Immediately. I warned her that she was doing serious damage to her children and her relationship with them. I said to her: "You are pushing them closer to their father."

I said: "God will vindicate you in His own way and in His own time."

He's Still Their Father

No matter how selfish, rotten, and sinful your ex was (and probably still is), he is still your children's father. They cannot see him the way you do. The position of wife and child are poles apart.

Especially for younger children, eighteen or less, dad is dad. He is a powerful, influential person in their lives. Their emotional well-being, their identity, their self-esteem, and their view of the world is shaped by their relationship with their father.

Your children are simply unable to quickly grasp the entire truth about their father. And even if they could, it would traumatize them and stunt their psychological and psychosocial development.

If you take the approach with younger children I cover in this chapter, you will protect your children and protect your relationship with them. And in time there is a good chance they will see the entire picture and realize the truth about dad.

What you want your children to eventually say is: "I love my father, but this is the truth about him."

Play the Long Game

With young children, you have to play the long game. In most cases, it will take years for your children to figure it all out.

Your long game begins by making three brief, direct, and honest statements of truth to your children.

These statements are to younger children, ages approximately eight to eighteen. Deliver these in order, about a week apart. Give the first statement, seven days later give the second, and seven days later give the third.

Put my words in these statements into your own words and adjust the language depending on the age of your children. Of course, insert the information that applies to your situation. It's best, if possible, to present the three statements in person to all your children in a group.

As you'll see, the approach I want you to take with your younger children is described in these statements.

Statement #1: The Truth About the Marriage and Divorce

"In our marriage, I made mistakes and your father made mistakes. We both are to blame for the marital problems. But, it's important that you know that the divorce was one hundred percent your father's fault. (here, list your ex's actions that ended the marriage. Not in detail, just the basic categories:

- Your father didn't want to be married to me anymore and he filed for divorce.
- Your father left home and was never going to come back.

- Your father was in a relationship with another woman.
- Your father called me names, criticized me constantly, got angry often, said terrible things to me, and refused to change.
- The Bible teaches that I had a right to file for divorce because your father would not stop abusing me.)

I will forgive your dad for hurting me so badly. I'm working on that now. It will take time. But forgiving him does not mean he and I will be friends. I'll do my best to get along with him for your sakes, but we won't be friendly.

We all need to heal and forgive, and make a new life after the divorce. The way to do that is to talk about these things. It's hard for me to talk about it and I know it's hard for you to talk about it. But we need to talk.

If I see you upset because of something your father said or did, I will ask you to talk about it.

If I hear about a lie that he told you, I will come to you and correct that lie with the truth.

If you want to talk to me about dad and the divorce, come to me anytime and we'll talk. Anytime.

When we have these talks, they will be completely private. I will tell no one what we talk about.

At some point, I may ask you to go with me to a Christian counselor so we can talk through all the pain and sadness of the divorce. And to talk about what life is like now, after the divorce."

Statement #2: The Truth About the Divorce Agreement

"Kids, I need to go over the part of the divorce agreement that talks about how your father and I will share time with you.

(here, cover the specific custody and time - sharing plan: which days of the week you will have them, and which days their father will have them, the Holiday schedule, school breaks and summer schedule...)

I will never try to interfere with your relationship with your father. That is between you and him. When it's your time to be with him, you can be with him. If you want to communicate with him when you are in my home, you can do it.

Dad's parents, Grandpa and Grandma____, will see you when you are with your father.

I will have as little contact with your father as possible. I won't talk to him in person or on the phone. I will only communicate via text or email.

When I have to be in the same place with him, I won't talk to him. I won't pretend to like him.

I will have my behavior standards in my home and your father will have his in his home. These standards will be different. All I can do is control what happens in my home.

I won't ask you what happened when you were with your father. You can tell me if you want and we can talk about it. I hope and pray that when you're with dad you will choose to follow God's rules and not sin.

If you ever want to talk about any of this, come to me anytime and we will talk."

Statement #3: The Truth About Life in Your New Home

"Because I am now a single parent, things will be very different in this home. I'll have less time and energy. I'll be more stressed and irritable. I ask you to please hang in there with me. I know it's hard on you too, so I will also hang in there with you.

I'll need more help from you to make this home work. You'll have to do more chores (detail these). You'll have to do your own laundry (tell them how often to do it). You'll have to do more food preparation and clean up after meals (give them specifics). You'll have to be more responsible for your schoolwork because I won't have the time to help you as much.

I will have friends and family (give the names) helping me with babysitting, driving you to school and your activities, and home repairs.

You may have fewer activities and sports because I won't be able to make it happen.

Your relationship with God is the most important thing in life to me. So, when you are with me, we'll all go to church. And, I'll lead a once a week family devotion time.

Here are the behavior standards I expect you to obey in this home (give standards). When you choose to follow my standards, you will be rewarded. When you choose to not follow my standards, there will be consequences." (read my book, Parenting is Hard and Then You Die, for a clear set of standards and reasonable rewards and consequences.)

The approach you must take with adult children after divorce is very different than the one with younger children. Let me show you what not to do and what to do with your adult children.

CHAPTER FOURTEEN

You and Your Adult Children

After your divorce, don't be surprised when your adult children do not want to hear the truth about their father. They may blame you for the divorce. Or, even if they don't blame you for the divorce, they won't care what caused the marriage to end.

Most adult children do not want to talk about the marriage and the divorce. They want to leave the past behind and start fresh with a relationship with each of you.

Here are the main reasons your adult children won't talk about the divorce:

- You protected them all along from the sinful, relationship-destroying behaviors of your ex.
- They didn't experience the wounds and trauma he inflicted on you.
- They have no reason to be angry with him.

- The divorce does not affect them as much because they are out of your home and living their own lives.
- It's easier to have a conflict-free relationship with dad than to face the truth about him.
- They don't want their children to be pulled into the problems between you and their father.
- Your ex has had plenty of time – years of their lives – to highlight your problems and convince them the divorce was your fault.

One Divorced Woman's Story

My client was married for over thirty years to an abusive man. He belittled her constantly, didn't spend time with her, would never open up and share personally with her, and ignored her needs.

He was a serial adulterer and had emotional and physical relationships with several women. He denied any adultery and was clever enough to leave no evidence.

He was a smooth, charming narcissist who enjoyed helping others. He served at their church for years and was loved and respected by the pastor and the church leaders.

During the marriage, my client didn't talk to her two daughters about his abusive behavior. She wanted to protect them from the pain she was going through. And, she wanted them to have a relationship with their father.

He spent years making her look bad to the daughters. He would deliberately get her very upset and angry and tearful. He'd stay calm and say to the girls: "mom's too sensitive," " mom is over-reacting," " mom has a temper," " mom's emotionally unstable."

When she came to me, she had finally divorced him to save herself. Her emotional and physical health were shot.

I recommended that she do my divorce recovery program, but she was obsessed with trying to get her adult daughters to see the truth about her abusive ex. She wanted them to understand the awful pain he had put her through.

She had gathered solid evidence of his adulterous affairs, but her daughters refused to look at it or talk about it. She got upset, pressed the issue, and looked crazy.

She tried to tell the girls about his abuse over the years, but they refused to listen. She got upset, pressed the issue, and looked crazy.

I told her to stop trying to convince her daughters that their father was abusive and she had a right to divorce him. I told her to drop it, never mention her ex to the girls again, and go through my divorce recovery program.

She didn't listen to me, so I stopped seeing her. Some time later, she came in to tell me she had continued to pressure her daughters to face the truth about their dad. They had ended all contact with her and cut her off from seeing her grandchildren.

She didn't look like the same person. She had aged at least twenty years. Her new identity was: "I was wronged by my ex-husband."

She still refused to follow my guidance. She had become a professional martyr seeking vindication. That was the last time I saw her.

Don't Be a Martyr

Don't end up like my client, with a driving need for your adult children to understand your pain and believe the divorce wasn't your fault. You'll look like a crazy, unstable person. You'll confirm all the negative things your ex has told them about you.

In your desperate effort to get them to see your ex's faults, all you will do is get them to see your faults. Who do you think they will blame? The calm, rational dad or the angry, emotional, bouncing off the walls mom?

Listen to me. Your adult children don't care about your mental pain and who was responsible for the divorce. If you try to make them care, you will lose them.

To build the best possible relationship with your adult children, here's what I want you to do.

Make a One-Time Statement

Deliver a one-time statement about the marriage and divorce to your adult children. Don't do it to the group. Present the same statement to each adult child separately. If you can't do it in person, FaceTime or Zoom is fine.

You can use the following example as a guide. Fill in the appropriate information that fits your specific situation.

"I will make a brief statement about the circumstances of the marriage and the divorce. It's important to me that you know the truth. I ask you to simply listen to me and not give any response at this time. Think and pray about what I said.

I will never bring up your father or these topics again, unless you reach out to me and want to talk about them. If you want to talk, I'll talk. If you don't, that's fine.

Our relationship does not depend in any way on how you see the marriage and divorce.

In the marriage, I made mistakes (list them in a general way). Your father also made mistakes (list these in a general way). I will take responsibility for my part in the marital problems, but I will take no blame for the divorce. Your father destroyed the marriage, not me.

I will forgive your father for the damage he did to me and to our marriage. I'm working on forgiveness now. But forgiveness does not mean I will be friendly to him. I don't trust him and will avoid contact with him as much as I can.

When I have to be at the same event with him, I'll be pleasant and civil, but I won't talk to him. Even though I will forgive him, I won't pretend to like him. I won't act as if he never hurt me.

What I want is to move on and build a great, close relationship with you and your children."

Build the Relationship with Your Children

The last line of your above statement says it all. After stating the truth in an honest, brief way, you drop the issue and work to build a great, close relationship with your adult children and your grandchildren.

Don't bring up your ex to your children or grandchildren. He has nothing to do with these relationships. You share your life with them and they share their lives with you. You show interest in what they're doing, you attend events with them, and you pray with them and for them.

Be Happy

Let your adult children know that you are happy in your new life. Let them see that you have moved on. You are at peace. You are doing well. Life is good.

When you have to be around your ex, project happiness and calmness and confidence. If you have to fake it until you are fully recovered from the divorce, fake it.

As you live a peaceful life and build your relationship with your adult children, they may see you differently and eventually see the truth about their father.

But if they never see the truth about him and about the divorce, who cares? That's not important. You'll be happy and close to them and that's all that counts.

I've shown you, at least in a basic way, how to deal with your children-younger and older- after the divorce. I'll show you now how to deal with your ex.

CHAPTER FIFTEEN

Managing Your Ex

Wouldn't it be great to never have contact of any kind with your ex after the divorce? No matter the circumstances of your divorce, he has wounded you as no one has ever wounded you.

But, you have children with him. So, obviously, you have to deal with him. No choice.

Expect Your Ex to be Difficult

I am making the assumption that your ex is difficult. It's a pretty safe assumption. A good relationship with an ex is a rare commodity. What's much more common – almost the rule – is an ongoing battle filled with anger, hurt, resentments, and childish games.

It's no surprise that your ex is difficult. That's why he is your ex.

Whatever type of person he was before the divorce is the type of person he will be after the divorce. Just as he did not change during the marriage, he won't change after it.

Expect the Worst

Your ex's selfish, abusive, and sinful behavior will take many forms:

- Showing up late to pick up the kids
- Keeping the kids longer than scheduled
- Changing plans at the last minute
- Bad mouthing you to the kids
- Not contributing enough financial support
- Trying to buy your kids' love
- Breaking promises
- Lying
- Ranting and raving on the phone, email, or text
- Asking you to do chores and errands that he should do

This is not a complete list of bad ex behaviors. I'm sure you could add to it. There are many potential reasons for this kind of abusive behavior:

- His desire to get revenge for how you hurt him
- His desire for power and control
- His desire to "win" by alienating the kids from you

- His desire to make you miserable because he's miserable
- He's just a mean, abusive dirtball

Management is the Key

The key to your ongoing "relationship" with your ex is to deal with him in a smart, strategic way that accomplishes these goals:

- Protects you
- Protects your children
- Limits the pain he can inflict on you

I call this operation *managing your ex.* It's a lot like handling a wild animal at the zoo. No matter what you do, he's still a wild animal. But, your careful management strategy keeps him from doing harm to you and others who have to be around him and in his cage.

Here's my Zookeeper Management Protocol:

How to Communicate with Him

As much as possible, communicate with him by text or email. These forms of communication are more impersonal and provide more protection. Plus, you will have a record of his communications.

He'll try to talk to you in person and by phone. Ignore those efforts.

Divorce means you can communicate with him any way you choose. And you choose text or email.

Stick to the Divorce Agreement

Follow the divorce agreement to the letter. If you make exceptions, your difficult ex will take full advantage. You will embolden him to want more and more concessions.

I recently saw a divorced mom who had given her ex whatever he wanted for a year after their divorce. He now was asking for outrageous concessions. I told her this was her own fault because she had been so accommodating. She was able to set new limits on him, but it was a lot harder than it should have been.

When you give in to his demands and allow him to act outside the divorce agreement, you lose respect and leverage. You are weak. You are a doormat and your ex will continue to wipe his feet on you.

Appeasement and compromise is what I call "feeding the beast". It will increase, not decrease, his self-serving behavior.

And don't give in when he's "nice" to you. He's only being nice to get what he wants. He's setting you up! Don't fall for his sweet, charming act.

Divorce means you don't have to do things his way anymore. You only have to do what the divorce agreement states.

When He Breaks the Divorce Agreement

Notice I used the word when. Your difficult spouse will break the divorce agreement multiple times. Pretty much whenever he feels like it.

When he breaks it (refuses to pick up the kids, refuses to give the kids back to you at the appointed time, refuses to pay you what he owes you….), make a record of the violation.

Note both his communication flaunting the agreement and your statements supporting it. This is evidence your attorney can use if you are forced to take him to court.

Every time he breaks the agreement, tell the kids what he's done.

If he consistently holds the kids and won't give them back to you for hours, don't hesitate to call the police. One of my clients called the police, showed them the divorce agreement, and they compelled her abusive ex to hand the kids over. He never held the kids back again.

If I've heard this complaint once, I've heard it a million times: "My ex promised to take the kids but at the last minute changed the plan and left me hanging."

You love your kids, but you need regular breaks from them. Plus, you do have a life and need to do things alone or with family and friends.

Always, always, always have a Plan B when your ex is scheduled to see the kids. Have a Plan B if it's only several hours or a weekend or a week. Have family, close friends, or babysitters lined up just in case your ex shafts you.

After he's changed the plan, it's a sweet moment when you text him: " Too bad you'll miss being with the kids. But I have a backup plan so it's all good. I'll still get my time off." Then sever the conversation.

He'll be beyond furious because the whole point of changing the plan at the last minute was to ruin your plan. He wasn't able to do that and, even better, you don't care. These are times to treasure.

Divorce means you don't have to tolerate his selfish, controlling behavior without providing consequences.

Don't get Sucked into His Sin and Stupidity

A crazy, bitter ex wants you to be miserable. In his nutball world, you have to be punished forever for your "crimes" against him. He feels this way even if he divorced you. Now, that's crazy!

Never, ever show him emotion. He wants an angry, hurt response from you. He wants to upset you and to know you're upset.

Never let him know he's getting to you. He's a bully and he's trying to get a reaction out of you. So, don't give him a reaction. Remain cool and reasonable.

He'll never stop trying to make you suffer, but your no response to his stupid, nasty comments will slow him down. When it's apparent you are not being affected by his stupid, nasty behavior, he won't do it as much.

Don't defend yourself. Don't waste another second of your life trying to reason with him. He's a fool and you don't reason with fools (Proverbs 14:7, 17:10, 23:9).

Feel free to vent your emotions with God and your Support Team. Go into your backyard and rip off a massive primal scream. But never let your ex know how upset he has made you.

When he sends you a long, rambling rant, scan it and only respond to the pertinent issues. Let's say he sends you an angry, abusive text about a bunch of past things and in it he mentions wanting to have the kids on a certain day. You only respond to his request/demand to have the kids on that day.

Divorce means you don't have to respond to his verbal abuse.

Just About Everything is Separate

You have every right to not be in his physical presence unless it's absolutely necessary. Even though you will forgive him, that doesn't mean you have to like him or be around him.

Just about every special event needs to be done separately: birthdays, holidays, vacations, get togethers with your family. Don't invite him to any of these events. Follow the divorce agreement and do these events separately.

When you and he both attend one of your children's activities, sit away from him and say nothing to him. The first few times, ask a family member or friend to go with you.

At certain events (weddings, funerals, birthdays of grandchildren), you'll have to be in the same room or building with him. Be happy, calm, and collected. Say nothing to him.

Divorce means you can do most events separately.

Coach Your Kids

If your ex is abusive, coach your kids how to deal with him. They need to practice responding to his lies, his attacks on you, his manipulation, his broken promises, his attempts to pump them for information about you, his efforts to win them over and get them to live with him full-time.

Tell your kids not to directly confront their father in his sinful behavior. That will cause him to retaliate against them and do real damage. Rather, it's smarter and safer for them to avoid him, to stay busy with other activities when with him, to never talk about you with him, and to come up with short, stock replies to his attempts to force them into awkward conversations:

"okay"

"fine"

"I don't know"

"I don't want to talk about that"

"Let me think about that"

They can switch the topic to him and what he's doing in his life and work and leisure activities. If he's a narcissist, he loves talking about himself.

Divorce means you don't have to leave your kids defenseless against his sinful behavior.

Don't Block Him from Your Social Media

Let him see how happy you are and how well you are doing. Let him see happy photos of you and the kids, you and your family, you and your friends, and you at church activities.

He'll hate seeing you happy and will engage with you less. And with a difficult ex, less is good.

Divorce means you can be happy and indirectly show him you're happy.

We've covered a lot of important ground to this point in the book. You're ready now to do the work of deeper healing.

CHAPTER SIXTEEN

How to Forgive

Divorce is one of the most devastating experiences that can happen in a person's life. It is a severe trauma. There is no question that you have PTSD (Post Traumatic Stress Disorder).

Healing from the trauma of your divorce is all about forgiveness. You have to forgive all those who wounded you in the divorce.

And, because your divorce has energized all your past unresolved pain, you have to forgive all those who wounded you significantly up to this point in your life.

I talked briefly about forgiveness in Chapter Ten. I made it clear that righteous anger is the first step in the process. Here, in the Healing Section, I'll guide you through the entire process of forgiveness.

The Church and Forgiveness

Many pastors, Christian counselors, and Christian leaders do not understand forgiveness. The traditional, and most popular, Christian advice goes like this: "Make the choice, right now, to forgive the person who harmed you."

That's it. That is the full extent of their teaching on forgiveness. There's just one problem with this advice: it doesn't work. It has never worked for anyone, though millions have tried it. It won't work for you, either.

I've been helping persons forgive for thirty-five years. I know how you forgive someone who has deeply wounded you.

In this Healing Section, I'm going to help you forgive everyone who has wounded you – in the divorce process and in your entire life.

Definition of Forgiveness

Here's my definition of forgiveness:

the difficult process by which, with

God's power, you heal from the

wounds a person inflicted on you

and leave those wounds in the past.

Difficult: it is brutal, messy, and awful work.

Process: it takes time and huge effort. Check out the Psalms of David and the book of Job.

With God's power: you can't forgive anyone in your own power. You forgive only with God's power.

Heal from the wounds: you face the trauma directly and take specific steps to deal with it.

A person inflicted on you: you always forgive a person, not a group of persons or a situation. And, you forgive one person at a time.

Leave these wounds in the past: based on the hard work you've done, you consciously decide to move on and not allow the wounds to impact your life.

There are three critical elements in true forgiveness:

Intellectual: you choose to do the hard work to forgive the person who wounded you.

Emotional: you do the work of healing from the trauma.

Spiritual: God enables you to do the work and release the pain caused by the person.

Release and Reconciliation Forgiveness

In this section (and in this book), I am only focusing on release forgiveness. Release forgiveness is a one-way process that does not involve the person who wounded you. You can completely forgive someone without mentioning to that person anything about the work you did to forgive him.

Reconciliation forgiveness is a two-way process that requires a healthy, honest response from the person who wounded you. To reconcile, the other person must admit fault, ask for your forgiveness, and be willing to help you heal from the wounds he inflicted on you.

There may be a few persons (not your ex!) with whom God directs you to attempt reconciliation forgiveness. There won't be many, if any, and you have to first accomplish release forgiveness anyway.

Your Past Pain List

Everyone has a past pain list. I have a past pain list. You have a past pain list. This is a list of persons who have significantly wounded you in the past.

I'm talking about major wounds, not minor. There's no need to do this hard work to forgive minor offenses. Who cares? You do have to deal with those who have seriously wounded you.

In the upcoming chapters, we'll deal first with those on your past pain list who caused you big pain in the marriage and in the divorce process: God, yourself, your ex, and others. These "others" could include family members, your adult children, friends, pastors, and counselors.

Then, we'll deal with all the others who wounded you in your life up to now. These could include your parents, a step-parent, siblings, previous spouses, previous intimate partners, friends, and anyone who caused you significant trauma.

Three Steps to Forgiveness

(These three steps are easy to communicate. They are very difficult to do. I urge you to work with a Christian therapist to accomplish the work of forgiveness. Find a therapist who is a solid Christian, licensed in your state, experienced, and who does not blame you for the divorce. Focus on the Family will have a list of Christian Therapists in your area. Check each therapist out carefully before you make your choice.)

These steps take time. How much time each step requires is variable. It depends on your personality, the level and complexity of the trauma, and the role of God in the process. Rely on God and your therapist for guidance.

For each person you need to forgive, you'll follow these steps.

Step One: Verbal Venting

You talk through the pain the person caused you with three persons: God, your Recovery Coach, and your Christian Therapist. This will usually not be one meeting with each of these three persons. It will be a series of venting conversations as the pain spills out of you.

You talk, in detail, about what happened. You feel and express your emotions without any filter or restrictions. You talk about the damage the person did to you. The impact on your life.

These venting sessions will jump start the healing process. They will connect you to your emotions. They will identify the specific memories God wants you to heal from and forgive.

You don't have to remember every hurt, even every major hurt, inflicted by the person. As you vent, God will give you the memories He wants to give you. It could be ten, eight, or four specific memories.

These memories will cover all your trauma with this person.

Step Two: The Throw Up Letter

When you're done verbally venting and know the memories to work on, you sit down and write a letter to the person who wounded you.

You can use pen and paper or type it into an electronic device. Although it is written directly to the person, you will not send it or share it in any direct way with that person. You will read it to God, your Recovery Coach, and your Therapist.

The Throw Up Letter is the written version of your verbal venting. You cover what happened, your emotions, the damage the person did to you, and the impact on your life.

It is raw, visceral, and completely honest. You hold back nothing. You make no excuses for the person. You show no understanding or compassion for the person. You offer not the slightest hint of forgiveness.

You let the person have it! You dump on the person the full weight of your pain as you write about the memories that surfaced in your verbal venting.

Once you've read this letter to your three support persons, I want you to put the person in an empty chair(remember the empty chair from Chapter Eleven?) and read it directly to him. If you want, you can have your Recovery Coach or Therapist in the room during the reading.

At this point, you will have some follow up conversations with God, your Recovery Coach, and your Therapist about the letter.

Step Three: The Forgiveness Letter

You're ready now to write the Forgiveness Letter to the person you are forgiving. Just as with the Throw Up Letter, you will not send this letter or share it in any direct way with the person. You will read it to God, your Recovery Coach, and your Therapist.

In the Forgiveness Letter, you include a brief summary of what happened and your emotions. Then, you correct the lies the trauma put into your head and make it clear you will no longer allow the wounds to impact your life. Finally, you close with words of forgiveness: "With God's power, I forgive you. I release all the pain to God and leave it in the past."

Once you've read this letter to your three support persons, put the person in the empty chair and read it directly to him. You can have a support team member in the room during this reading.

If you feel the need to have a few follow up talks with your support team members about the letter, do it. Then, for closure, I want you to burn the Throw Up Letter and the Forgiveness Letter.

In the following chapters, I'll give examples of these letters so you know how to do them.

Forgiveness will clean out all your unresolved pain, eliminate your false guilt, and give you the freedom to move forward in your new life.

Let's get to the work of forgiveness.

CHAPTER SEVENTEEN

You and God

My client: "I have something to tell you. I did something very bad and I am so ashamed of myself."

Me: "Go ahead and tell me. We'll work through it together."

My Client: "I prayed a million times to God, asking Him to change my husband and save my marriage. I was sure God would do that for me. For my children. When God didn't do that and I got divorced, I lost trust in God. I was so angry with God. I yelled and screamed at God. I took my Bible and tore it in half. Am I going to Hell now?"

Me: "No, you're not going to Hell. First, once you believe that Jesus died for your sins and rose from the dead, you have a relationship with God that is unbreakable. Second, your intense emotions and honesty with God are perfectly normal and healthy reactions. God wants you to be honest with Him. He can take it."

It's Okay to Wrestle with God

It's not only okay to wrestle with God, it is necessary. Healing and forgiveness begin with working through your issues with God.

Wrestling with God is super awkward and scary. It doesn't seem right. But I'm telling you, it is right. As I told my client, God wants you to be honest with Him.

Join the Club

You know why I believe that being honest with God by venting pain with Him and asking questions of Him is healthy? Because of all the persons in the Bible who were honest with God.

I could give you many examples of persons in the Bible who wrestled with God, but here are seven:

Job (the Book of Job): God took everything from the most righteous man on earth. Job spent forty-two chapters working through the trauma and his issues with God.

David (many of the Psalms): David (a man after God's own heart) expressed a host of painful emotions with God: anger, frustration, fear, desperation, hopelessness, grief. He questioned God over and over.

Solomon (book of Ecclesiastes): Solomon, the King of Israel, questioned the purpose and meaning of life. In doing so, he questioned God because God created human life.

Jacob (Genesis 32:22-32): Jacob, son of Isaac and a patriarch of Israel, literally wrested with God for one entire night. His stubbornness, pride, and selfishness were expressed in the fight.

Habakkuk (book of Habakkuk): Habakkuk, a prophet of God, questioned God in two main areas: why did God allow wicked people to prosper and why did God use the evil Babylonians to punish God's people?

Paul (2 Corinthians 12:7-9): The apostle Paul, one of the godliest men who ever lived, struggled with God over "a thorn in my flesh" that God gave to him.

Jesus (Luke 22:42-44; Mark 15:33-34): Jesus, the son of God and who was God Himself, asked God the Father to spare Him the crucifixion. And, just before He died, Jesus asked God why He had rejected Him.

For every person above, God allowed their honest expression of pain and their questions. For all seven, their direct and honest wrestling with God led to a stronger and more intimate relationship with Him.

You and God

Just as these seven Biblical persons did, you need to be honest with God. You need to talk to God about the pain of your divorce and His role in it.

Your honesty with God will re-connect you to Him. It will strengthen your relationship with Him. It will create a closer relationship with Him. And, it will enable you to use His power to forgive yourself, your ex, and everyone else who has harmed you.

Follow My Template

I want you to follow my three-step Template for Forgiveness I covered in the previous chapter: Verbal Venting, the Throw Up Letter, and the Forgiveness Letter.

Let me be clear. You do not forgive God. He didn't do anything wrong. But you do have to be honest with Him and work things out with Him.

Verbal Venting

Verbally vent all your questions for God and all your emotions about God's role in your divorce to your Recovery Coach and your Christian Therapist.

Let it all out. Don't hold back anything. God wants you to do it. These venting sessions may take a few weeks.

The Throw Up Letter

Once your venting is over, you'll know what to put in your Throw Up Letter to God. It will feel strange writing a letter to God, but do it anyway.

Here's a brief section of one client's Throw Up Letter to God.

Dear God, I am furious with You

because You didn't save my marriage.

You could have, but You didn't. I

begged You to help me, to change my

husband, but all I got was silence.

Why didn't You stop me from marrying

him? Why didn't You answer all my

prayers about my marriage? Why

didn't You stop my ex-husband from committing adultery? Why didn't You change my husband? Why didn't You stop the adultery and bring him back to me? Why do You hate me so much? Why are You punishing me? Why didn't You give me a better divorce settlement? Why didn't You protect my children?

Read your completed letter to God, your Recovery Coach, and your Therapist.

The Forgiveness Letter

Here's a brief section of one client's Forgiveness Letter to God.

Dear God, Thank You for allowing me to be totally honest with You. My divorce was and is very painful for me. And my children. I may not ever fully understand why You allowed the divorce. But what I do know is that

You love me and You don't make
mistakes.
I don't blame You anymore for
the divorce. I blame my ex-husband.
It was his sin and refusal to stop his
sin that ended our marriage.
I feel like I'm back on track in my
relationship with You. I feel closer
to You than I ever have in my life.
I know You have good things in
store for me.

Read your completed letter to God, your
Recovery Coach, and your Therapist.

The Way Forward

As you wrestle with God, I want you to hold
onto the truth that nothing – absolutely nothing –
can separate you from the love of God in Jesus
(Romans 8:35-39).

Once you have worked things out with God,
you can move on to working things out with
yourself.

CHAPTER EIGHTEEN

You and Yourself

My Client: "I know that God has forgiven me for my mistakes in the marriage. I know that the divorce was my ex-spouse's fault, not mine. But I don't feel forgiven by God. I still feel tremendous guilt for the divorce."

Me: "You are a lot harder on yourself than God is. You are continuing to punish yourself for sins that God has forgiven and forgotten. What you're feeling is false guilt. Intellectual acceptance of the truth isn't enough. You have to take the right action steps to emotionally accept the truth."

"Once you have directly faced your mistakes as a wife and admitted your responsibility for each one to God, you will feel forgiven by God. And once you feel forgiven by God, you can forgive yourself and all others who caused you pain in the divorce."

Sources of False Guilt

It's common – in fact, almost everyone does it – for divorced persons to feel guilt for their divorce for years. It's easy to focus on your marital mistakes and continue to blame yourself for the divorce.

Your ex, who is one hundred percent to blame for the divorce, feels no guilt at all. Doesn't seem fair, does it?

Your false guilt is a form of denial. "If only I had been a better wife, we wouldn't have gotten divorced." "If only I had gotten us to counseling earlier, we wouldn't have gotten divorced." "If only I had ___ fill in the blank ___, we wouldn't have gotten divorced."

This kind of distorted thinking keeps you in a never-ending cycle of false guilt and false shame. The misery, however, is real.

Others certainly contribute to your false guilt. Your ex-spouse will enthusiastically blame you for the divorce. He has to justify his sin and look good. He is thrilled in his nasty little mind that you feel guilty for the divorce *he* caused.

I wouldn't be surprised if your pastor and even your Christian counselor hold you responsible, at least in part, for the divorce. Plenty of well-meaning but clueless "helpers" blame both spouses for the divorce.

As I have stated before, you are one hundred percent responsible for your mistakes in the marriage. Every spouse makes mistakes that harm the marriage. You are zero percent responsible for the divorce.

The key to emotionally accepting this truth is embracing God's forgiveness for your mistakes in the marriage.

Loving Yourself

God wants you to love yourself. Read the words of Jesus in Matthew(Chapter 22: 36-39):

> "Teacher, which is the greatest
>
> commandment in the law? Jesus
>
> replied: 'Love the Lord your God
>
> with all your heart and with all
>
> your soul and with all your mind.
>
> This is the first and greatest
>
> commandment.
>
> And the second is like it: Love your
>
> neighbor as yourself.'"

It is essential to the Christian life to love God with everything you have in you. It's equally essential to love yourself in a healthy, God-honoring way.

By accepting God's forgiveness for your mistakes in the marriage, you are loving yourself. With your false guilt gone, you can forgive yourself and others. And, most importantly, get yourself and your issues out of the way so you can fully love God.

The Truth About Forgiveness

One verse sums up all you need to know about the intellectual part of God's forgiveness:

If we confess our sins, He is

faithful and just and will forgive

us our sins and purify us from

all unrighteousness. (I John 1:9)

All you have to do is admit your sins to God and He certainly forgives you.

To fully accept the truth in I John 1:9 and experience God's forgiveness, you have to do the emotional work.

Follow My Template

Let's follow my three-step Forgiveness Template and get rid of your false guilt once and for all.

Verbal Venting

Talk through – with God, your Recovery Coach, and your Christian Therapist – all the sins and mistakes you made in the marriage and in the divorce process. Identify each sin and describe its impact on your ex and the marriage.

Don't be general. Be specific and detailed. Do not justify your behavior. Own it.

The Throw Up Letter

This letter will be to your ex, though he'll never see it. In a sense, this letter and the Forgiveness Letter are also to God because He is the One whose forgiveness is important.

You don't need your ex's forgiveness. Not that you'd get it, anyway.

Here is a brief section of one client's Throw Up Letter to her ex.

Bob, part of my healing and

forgiveness process is admitting my

sins and mistakes in our marriage. I take no blame for the divorce. That is entirely your fault. But I do take complete blame for my sins in the marriage. I tolerated your anger and did nothing to stop it. I didn't demand apologies after your outbursts. I didn't provide any consequences. So, I was an enabler of your anger and that was my fault.

I did not give you enough physical affection. I know it was important to you, but I didn't work on this issue hard enough. I know this hurt you, but I didn't care enough to fix it. That was my fault.

I focused too much on the kids, I can see that now. Their needs came first and you got the leftovers. Many days, I had no time or energy for you.

That was hurtful and wrong and it was my fault.

I spent too much money and never stuck to the budget. I have no excuse. I know my spending stressed you and hurt you. That was my fault.

Read your completed letter to God, Your Recovery Coach, and your Therapist.

The Forgiveness Letter

Here is a brief section of one client's Forgiveness Letter to her ex.

Bob, I made many mistakes in our marriage. I can see now that my behavior was wrong and it pushed you away from me. I offer no excuses. What I did and said was wrong. I own my mistakes and the damage I caused.

I am sorry for how I hurt you.

I am sorry for the pain I caused.

I am sorry for everything I did
to harm our marriage.

I don't need your forgiveness
and I won't ask you for it. But
I do need God's forgiveness
and I am asking for that now.

I believe God has forgiven me
for all my sins in the marriage.

Jesus died for all my sins
including those I committed in
our relationship.

I will not feel any more guilt for
my mistakes in the marriage. I
will not feel any more guilt for
the divorce.

I'm moving on with God's total
forgiveness.

Read your completed letter to God, your Recovery Coach, and your Therapist.

A Final Prayer

I recommend, to achieve emotional and spiritual closure, a brief prayer accepting God's forgiveness for all your sins in the marriage. You can pray this alone or with your Coach or Therapist. You can use words like these:

> Dear God, I have admitted to
>
> my ex-spouse and to You all my
>
> sins in my marriage. I am sorry
>
> for my sins. I thank You for Your
>
> forgiveness and accept Your
>
> forgiveness. With Your forgiveness,
>
> I don't have to feel any guilt for my
>
> mistakes as a spouse or for the
>
> divorce.

You're doing well. You're on track in the healing and forgiveness journey. It's time to forgive your ex. This work won't be pleasant, but it's necessary.

CHAPTER NINETEEN

You and Your Ex

It's very easy to get stuck in the divorce recovery process. That's why God made Christian psychologists. My job is to make sure you don't get stuck. Or, if you're already stuck, to get you unstuck.

One of the main ways a divorced spouse gets stuck is by not forgiving the ex. If you don't do the work – and it's hard work – to heal and forgive your ex, a lot of bad things happen to you:

- Your unresolved pain and trauma remain inside of you and never go away.
- You will never be released from your ex, but will remain traumatically bonded to him for the rest of your life.
- You will be bitter, resentful, angry, depressed, and anxious.
- Your unresolved pain will attack your body and cause serious physical damage.
- Your unresolved pain and trauma will transfer to every one of your close relationships.

- Because you haven't forgiven your ex, you violate God's law (Matthew 18:21-35) and will be estranged from Him.

There is no such thing as partial forgiveness. You don't sort of forgive your ex. You either do the work and completely forgive him, or you don't do the work and you don't forgive him.

I don't want all these awful consequences for you, and God certainly doesn't.

You have worked out your issues with God concerning the divorce. You have owned responsibility for your sins in the marriage and accepted God's forgiveness. Now, you're ready to heal from the wounds your spouse inflicted on you and forgive him.

Let's do my Forgiveness Template.

Verbal Venting

Have you ever seen the operation of a firehose? The spray of water is pressurized and intense and powerful. It takes a strong person to maintain control of the gushing torrent of water.

The rush of water is necessary to put out the fire and save lives.

I want you to vent like a firehose. No holding back. No sympathy or understanding for your ex. For years, you stuffed your emotions and your pain in order to cope and survive in the marriage.

You couldn't be honest with your ex about how you were really feeling. About how he was hurting you time after time. He would ignore you, shut you down, talk over you, or make you suffer for speaking truth.

So, you have a huge backlog of pain and anger and hurt and other emotions to get out of your system. As you verbally vent all the pain connected to your ex – with God, your Recovery Coach, and your Therapist – you will put out the fire inside you and save yourself.

The Verbal Venting step may last a while. Take all the time you need. Don't rush it. I want you to open up the firehose and get all the pain out.

Talk about all the times:

- He belittled you
- He controlled you
- He embarrassed you
- He ignored you

- He lectured you
- He wounded you
- He rejected you
- He turned the kids against you
- He lied to you
- He blamed you
- He abused you
- He _____

Free associate, open up your mind, and let the pain flow.

From all the painful, traumatic memories, choose six to eight and focus on them. I want you to verbally describe these specific memories in detail: what happened, when it happened, what he did and said, and the impact on you.

What you are doing is reliving these six to eight memories. God will make these memories cover all the pain and trauma you experienced from your ex.

The Throw Up Letter

Once your Verbal Venting has run its course and you have talked through the painful memories, I want you to write your ex the Throw

Up Letter. (You won't send him this letter or the Forgiveness Letter.)

This will be a brutal, honest, detailed, raw, no holds barred, no compassion and no forgiveness offered account of the six to eight memories you identified in the Verbal Venting step.

Here's one memory a client of mine wrote as part of her Throw Up Letter to her ex.

> Bob (*it's always Bob*), Your deceptive handling of our finances caused me terrible pain. The late payments of bills, running up the credit card balance, and borrowing money from my family were bad enough.
>
> But, the capper was the big "investment" you made behind my back. Your friend thought it was a good idea. Well, your friend is an idiot and so are you for listening to him.
>
> 75,000 dollars! You did everything

behind my back. No discussion. You
got the loan secretly and made
the investment secretly. When it
failed and you lost all 75K, you still
didn't tell me. You are a liar and
a deceiver!
I only found out because you had
to tell me. You couldn't repay
the loan and you couldn't pay our
other bills.
I was shocked and furious! What
kind of a husband would do this to
his wife? I'll tell you – a stupid,
selfish, greedy, foolish man!
I was hurt and sad and crushed.
Overwhelmed with fear about
our family's security and future.
I was not as angry as I should have
been back then, but I'm angry now
as I write these words.

You not only lied to me for months about the investment, you had the nerve to blame me!

You said I didn't appreciate the financial stress you were under because I didn't work and bring income into the home. We agreed I'd stay home and take care of the kids!

You said if we'd discussed the investment, I would have said no. Well, of course, I would have said no! Anyone with a brain would have said no!

You said I wouldn't have understood the investment. What I understand is that you cost us 75,000 dollars, you bonehead! It was you who didn't understand the investment!

Bob, that night you destroyed my

trust in you. You destroyed my
respect for you. And my love for
you. To top it off, you weren't
even sorry for what you did. You
were only sorry you got caught.

Read your completed letter to God, your
Recovery Coach, and your Therapist.

The Forgiveness Letter

Here is a brief section of this same client's
Forgiveness Letter to her ex. I've included her
follow-up comments about the financial memory
and some other material.

Bob…I want to you to know that
your 75K investment was entirely
your fault. How could I be at
fault when I knew nothing about
it?
I refuse to feel guilt for your sinful
choices. It's clear to me now that
the 75K mistake revealed a lot
about your character and your

feelings for me.

You are a liar and a deceiver
and a manipulator. And
incredibly selfish. That foolish
investment was all for you, not
for me.

You love only yourself. All my
efforts and attempts to love
you and reason with you were
a waste of time.

I am through allowing you to
impact my life. You certainly
harmed me during our marriage,
but I will not allow you to
continue to harm me.

I will no longer believe the lies
you made me believe about
myself. I am a good, smart, and
capable woman. I am a good mom.
I was the best wife I could be.

I have expressed and worked through the pain you caused me during our marriage and divorce. I am moving on from the wounds and misery you inflicted on me. I am free from you and can live the life God wants me to live.

I don't wish any harm to come to you. In fact, I hope you work on your issues and build a close relationship with God. But, that's up to you.

With God's power, I forgive you. I release all the pain you caused me to God and leave it all in the past.

Read the completed letter to God, your Recovery Coach and your Therapist.

Now that you've done your work with God, Yourself, and your Ex, you're prepared for the final part of the forgiveness process.

It's time to forgive everyone else who has significantly harmed you – in the divorce process and in your life.

CHAPTER TWENTY

You and Everybody Else

You've taken a huge step forward in your healing by following my three step Template with God, Yourself and your Ex. But you're not done yet.

You've got more healing to do.

This is your opportunity to clean out all the unresolved pain others have caused you in your life – from childhood until today.

I want you to start with those who harmed you in the divorce process. Then, I want you to deal with all those who harmed you in your life up to now.

The Same Three Step Forgiveness Template

Follow my same Template: Verbal Venting, The Throw Up Letter, and the Forgiveness Letter.

Facing and cleaning out the pain these persons caused you will take time. Several months at least. But, when you're done, you're done.

The unresolved pain and its impact on you will be gone. You'll be healthy, all caught up on forgiveness, and ready to move into your new life with confidence.

Past Pain List for the Divorce

Here is one divorced client's past pain list for her divorce (she did my three step Template with all these persons):

My pastor: He blamed me for the marriage problems. Instead of confronting my sinning husband, he urged me to love him more. Terrible advice.

Two church leaders: They were gutless and refused to confront my husband with his sin.

My first Christian Therapist: He ignored my husband's sin and taught us communication skills. Waste of time.

My former best friend: She stayed friends with my husband because she didn't want to "play favorites." She told my husband things I told her in confidence.

My adult children: They sided with my husband, believed his lies, and blamed me for the divorce.

Past Pain List for All Others

Here is this same client's past pain list for the others who did significant damage to her in her life (she did my three step Template with all these persons):

My father: He neglected me. He spent very little time with me. He favored my brother. He never said I love you to me.

My stepmom: She was critical, cold, and rejecting. She favored her kids over me.

Older neighbor boy: He sexually abused me four times. I never told anyone.

My previous husband: My husband before this ex emotionally abused me on a regular basis. I was never good enough for him. And, he was a chronic porn user.

Once she did her work with these persons who wounded her, both in the divorce and in her life, she was ready to live life to the fullest.

She was ready to date again. Once you've done this past pain work, you'll be ready to date again, too.

CHAPTER TWENTY-ONE

How to Spot a Loser

When you're ready to date, you will be in good shape because of the work you've done in my divorce recovery process.

Healthy persons tend to choose healthy partners.

But I want to make sure you choose the best partner to date and to marry. You've got to get this one right.

You don't want to make a mistake. You want to find the person who will make a great spouse for the rest of your life.

In this chapter, I cover the types of losers you must avoid. In the next chapter, I cover the profile of the person you can date and marry with confidence.

My List of Losers

Here's a list of losers you must stay away from at all costs. Each one has a red flag – actually, a red blanket – attached to the back of his(or her) head.

If you come across one of these losers, immediately run – screaming your head off – away from him down the opposite side of the street. And don't look back.

Mr. I'm Not a Christian

This should be the first question you ask a *potential* date: "Do you have a personal relationship with God, through His Son, Jesus Christ?" If he pauses, don't date him. If he says no, don't date him.

If you marry someone who isn't a Christian, you will never be able to spiritually bond. So, you will never truly be "one flesh" (Genesis 2:24).

Mr. I'm a Weak Christian

If your potential date says he is a Christian, follow up with these questions:

- When did you become a Christian?
- Are you growing in your relationship with Jesus?
- What are you doing to grow in this relationship?
- Do you regularly attend a local church?
- Do you have a daily quiet time in which you pray and read the Bible?

- Do you tithe to your local church?

A weak Christian may always remain weak. You want a partner who has a strong, growing relationship with Jesus right now.

Mr. I'm a Momma's Boy

He is way too attached to his momma. He calls her just about every day. He can't make a move without her advice and approval. She is his top priority, which means you will never be.

Mr. I'm Tied to My Ex

He's way too attached to his ex. It's hard to tell they're divorced, because he does everything her way. She makes all the decisions about their kids. She plans and controls all family activities. She runs his life. If you marry him, you are marrying her, too.

Mr. I Won't Do Conflict

He refuses to talk through conflicts with you. He avoids conflict like the plague and, when it does surface, he shuts down and will not deal with it. Dump this gutless loser, because you have to work through all conflicts in a relationship.

Mr. I Have a Temper

He blows up unpredictably and it's not pretty. He raises his voice, rants, and has a fit when something bothers him. And there's a long list of things that bother him. If he does this anger routine when you're dating, it will get even worse if you marry him.

Mr. I'm Always Right

He is a know it all who somehow always has the best solution to a problem. It's like dating the Google search engine because he knows everything. Your opinion doesn't count. Unless you are okay with always doing everything his way, lose his contact information and move on.

Mr. I Won't Talk

He won't talk personally. He won't share his emotions. He won't share his opinions. It's impossible to have a deep conversation with him. Do not think he'll suddenly start talking after marriage. You might as well marry a couch because at least it's good for something.

Mr. My Past is a Secret

He won't talk about his childhood. He won't talk about his family. He won't talk about his previous girlfriends. He won't talk about his previous marriages. He's in the CIA or an alien from another planet. Either way, get rid of this mystery man.

Mr. I Can't Keep a Job

He has gone from job to job to job. Amazingly, each job loss was not his fault. He's been on unemployment more than he's worked at a job. If you value financial security, stop dating this loser.

Mr. I'm in a Custody Battle

He's in a vicious, all-out battle with his ex over their kids. His life, and now your life, is consumed with attorneys, court appearances, and legal costs. I don't care how cute his kids are or how big a witch his ex is, get away from him. These custody battles never end.

Mr. I Want to Be a Citizen

He desperately wants to become an American citizen. You are a citizen, so by marrying you he will have a path to his citizenship. Is he truly in love with you or in love with the citizenship you can give him? There's no way to tell. Give him the number of an immigration attorney and walk away.

Mr. I Am Possessive

He loves you so much that he wants you all to himself. He asks you to cut off your family and your friends. He will graciously allow you to have limited time with those close to you. But always on his terms. Flee from this controlling jerk. After marriage he'll try to control every aspect of your life.

Mr. I Was Not at Fault

He accepts no blame for the failure of his previous marriage or marriages. He tells you all the marital problems were the fault of his ex. All of them. Guess who he will blame when you two have marital problems? Move on and move on quickly.

Mr. I'm Still Married

It doesn't matter if he's in a divorce process. He's still married. It doesn't matter if he's separated from his wife. He's still married. By dating him, you are committing adultery. That's not a great way to begin a relationship.

Confess your sin to God, and say goodbye to this husband.

Mr. I Am an Active Addict

He is currently struggling with an addiction: alcohol, drugs, sex, gambling, or spending. He says he wants to get into recovery. Let someone else take on this project.

Mr. I Want to Live Together

He loves you, but doesn't want to marry you. At least, not yet. He wants to live with you and see how things go. Listen to me. He doesn't love you. He's not committed to you. Living together is sin (I Thessalonians 4:3; Hebrews 13:4) and you'll both pay a high price for it.

Here's the price you'll pay by living together without marriage:

- A loss of respect for each other
- A loss of trust for each other
- A loss of love for each other
- A loss of closeness with God
- A loss of the ability to spiritually bond
- A loss of God's blessing on your relationship
- A loss of your relationship

Couples who live together tend to not get married. Couples who live together and get married get divorced at a higher rate.

When a man (or woman) asks you to live together without marriage, yell "Look behind you!" When he turns around to look, run the other way.

Okay, this is who you shouldn't date. Now, I'm going to give you a profile of the person you want to date and potentially marry.

CHAPTER TWENTY-TWO

How to Spot a Winner

I've gone over the characteristics of a loser. Here are the characteristics of a winner. When you find a person who fits the following profile, you can have total confidence to date him and, if God leads you, to marry him.

He is Physically Attractive

This may seem like a no-brainer, but I've counseled divorced persons who were dating partners for whom they had no physical attraction. I said *were* because I told them to break up.

Physical attraction isn't the only factor in choosing a mate, but it has to be on the list. If you don't immediately have physical attraction, you won't develop it later. It's either there or it isn't there. So, if you don't have the va-va-voom for someone, vamoose (vamoose means "I'm outta here").

He is a Godly Man

He has a relationship with Jesus Christ and is growing in that relationship. He attends his own church regularly. He tithes to his church. He has a daily quiet time in which he prays and reads the Bible.

He also freely shares his spiritual life with you. He prays with you. He has spiritual conversations with you. He talks to you about the victories and struggles in his spiritual life.

He genuinely wants to help you grow in your relationship with Jesus. He doesn't follow you, he leads you spiritually. He makes sure you two attend church and pray and talk about your spiritual lives.

You're thinking: "Are there any guys like this out there?" Not many, but they are out there. Pray that God guides you to one.

He Talks to you on a Deeper Level

Physical chemistry is important, but emotional chemistry is critical. This man actually talks to you and shares his emotions and thoughts. He listens to you and has empathy for your emotions and problems.

Your conversations are fun and open and lead to deeper levels of emotional intimacy.

Most men will have a delay in expressing deeper things, but *he* will get back to you and give you the personal information you need to hear.

He Deals Directly with Conflict

He doesn't enjoy conflict (who does?), but he is man enough to talk through every conflict with you. He listens to you share your point of view and emotions and respects both. He shares his point of view and his emotions in a reasonable, adult way.

He stays with the conflict conversation until you feel satisfied. He works with you to make a decision and then sticks to that decision. He is willing to compromise.

When you want to talk about a difficult, awkward topic, he is willing to have that conversation.

He gets angry, but does not lose control. He says "I'm sorry" when he does or says something to hurt you. He admits his mistakes and works to correct them.

He Talks about His Past

He is open and honest with you about his past: his childhood, his family, his previous romantic relationships, and his previous marriages. He tells you, in detail, about his past and the pain he has suffered.

He tells you how others have wounded him. He tells you how he has wounded others. He admits the mistakes he has made in his previous romantic relationships and marriages, and how he has worked on these mistakes.

He wants you to meet his family and friends.

He is willing to read this book and, with you in support, go through all my divorce recovery steps.

He Treats His Kids Well

He is a loving father who is crazy about his kids. He works hard to spend time with them and meet their needs. He does not spoil them. When they disobey, he applies reasonable consequences.

When it's clear that you two are serious and marriage is on the table, he elevates you above his children. You become the most important human person in his life.

His Friends are Normal

You can tell a lot about a person by the people he hangs around. His friends are normal, emotionally healthy Christians. There are no alcoholics, drug addicts, or emotionally unstable persons in his inner circle. There is no drama in his personal life and relationships.

He has a Good Career

He has a solid job history, a good career, and is a hard worker. Not a workaholic, but a hard worker. He has a budget, spends reasonably, and has money in savings.

He drives a Porsche. Kidding. Whatever he drives, he takes care of his vehicle. And he doesn't drive like a maniac.

He is Focused on Meeting Your Needs

A big part of love is having a partner who works hard to meet your needs. He identifies your needs and meets them. If he can't meet a need, he'll tell you why.

He wants you to be happy and to feel loved, so often he'll do the things you want to do. If you want to go to a certain restaurant, he'll go. If you want to see a certain movie, he'll watch it with you. If you want to go to a craft fair, he'll go (now that's real love!).

And he does what you want with a great attitude. He gets to be with you, so he doesn't care what you do.

There are times – and should be – when he makes it clear he wants to do a certain activity. But most of the time, he's happy to do what you want to do.

He's Liked by Your People

Your family and friends like him. They think he is good for you. And, he gets along with your people. He is fine with you spending time with your people – alone or with him.

He is Good with Premarital Counseling

He is willing to go to premarital counseling with you. He wants the relationship to be strong and healthy prior to marriage. He is in no rush to marry you. He isn't stalling, he just wants you two to be ready.

He is willing to go through my book, *Honey, We Need to Talk,* with you as part of your premarital preparation.

No Speed Dating

You've heard of speed dating. Well, I strongly recommend slow dating. Take your time. Make sure you have a godly, solid, honest, and emotionally healthy person on your hands.

Do not settle. Do not rush into a new relationship.

Look for a person that fits the profile in this chapter. He or she is out there. Pray that God will bring you two together.

Now, a final word.

CHAPTER TWENTY-THREE

Hit the Re-set Button

Well, here we are at the end of our journey. It's not been an easy one, has it? My divorce recovery steps are tough. Very tough. And demanding.

But they work. Over my thirty-five years of practice, I have seen God use these steps to heal divorced persons and give them a re-set in their lives.

I want you to add your story of divorce recovery to the many stories of recovery I've been involved with over the years.

Take heart and courage from these verses:

God is our refuge and strength,

an ever present help in trouble.

(Psalm 46:1)

God is with you in this time of trouble.

He gives strength to the weary

and increases the power of the

weak. (Isaiah 40:29)

God will give you the strength and the power to complete my divorce recovery plan.

> Forget the former things; do
>
> not dwell on the past. See, I
>
> am doing a new thing! Now
>
> it springs up; do you not
>
> perceive it? I am making a
>
> way in the desert and
>
> streams in the wasteland.
>
> (Isaiah 43:18-19)

God will help you move on from your divorce, get a re-set, and enjoy a brand new life.

A very good life.

ADDITIONAL RESOURCES

Other books by David Clarke

My Spouse Wants Out: How to Get Angry, Fight Back, and Save Your Marriage with William G. Clarke

Married But Lonely: Seven Steps You Can Take With or Without Your Spouse's Help with William G. Clarke

I Don't Want a Divorce: A 90-Day Guide to Saving Your Marriage with William G. Clarke

What to Do When Your Spouse Says, "I Don't Love You Anymore": An Action Plan to Regain Confidence, Power and Control

Enough is Enough: How to Leave an Abusive Relationship with William G. Clarke

I Destroyed My Marriage: How to Win Your Spouse Back with William G. Clarke

The Secret to Becoming Soulmates: A Couple's Devotional Journey to Spiritual Intimacy with William G. Clarke

Kiss Me Like You Mean It: Solomon's Crazy in Love How-to Manual

A Marriage After God's Own Heart

I'm Not Ok and Neither Are You: The 6 Steps to Emotional Freedom

The Top Ten Most Outrageous Couples of the Bible: And How Their Stories Can Revolutionize Your Marriage with William G. Clarke

Men Are Clams, Women are Crowbars: The Dos and Don'ts of Getting Your Man to Open Up with William G. Clarke

Parenting is Hard and Then You Die: A Fun but Honest Look at Raising Kids of All Ages Right with William G. Clarke

Honey, We Need to Talk: Get Honest and Intimate in Ten Essential Areas with William G. Clarke

To order Dr. Clarke's books, set up an in-person or telephone advice session, schedule a marriage intensive, access his podcast and YouTube Channel, or schedule a seminar, go to:

davideclarkephd.com

1-888-516-8844

Or

davideclarkephd@gmail.com

ABOUT THE AUTHORS

David E. Clarke, Ph.D., is a Christian psychologist, speaker, and the author of fifteen books including, *I Don't Want a Divorce, My Spouse Wants Out,* and *Enough is Enough: How to Leave an Abusive Relationship.* He is a graduate of Dallas Theological Seminary in Dallas, Texas, and Western Conservative Baptist Seminary in Portland, Oregon. He has been in private practice for more than thirty years. He and his Blonde, Sandy, live in Tampa, Florida. They have four children and four grandchildren.

William G. Clarke, M.A., has been a marriage and family therapist for over thirty years. He is a graduate of the University of Southern California in Los Angeles, California, and the California Family Study Center in Burbank, California, where he earned the master's degree. With his wife, Kathleen, he served for nine years with Campus Crusade for Christ(now CRU). He is the founder of the Marriage and Family Enrichment Center in Tampa, Florida.